Praise for *Extraordinary Awakenings*

"Steve Taylor's brilliant new book introduces us to individuals who have experienced traumas and crises and have come out the other end deeply transformed and spiritually awakened. What I love most about this book is how clearly he outlines the process underlying these positive transformations. This can help us all with the crises and traumas of our own lives. Such a wonderful book!"

— **Phil Borges**, photographer and filmmaker, codirector of *Crazywise*

"A powerful and inspiring book that shows that the most difficult moments of life can also be the most transformational. The profoundly moving stories show how resilient human beings can become and how much potential lies inside us."

— **Scott Barry Kaufman**, founder and director of the Center for the Science of Human Potential and author of *Transcend: The New Science of Self-Actualization*

"In crystal-clear prose, Steve Taylor offers practical wisdom on how to transform and transcend life's inevitable turmoil. Taylor is a remarkable guide — sure-footed and calm — through the startling transformations that individuals sometimes undergo when facing death (their own or someone else's), being challenged by addictions, or experiencing the loss of what seems central to their identity. Taylor shows that when the ego attachments we take for granted are irretrievably broken, they can be replaced by a more encompassing and far more fulfilling sense of self, bringing with it tranquility and transcendence. As with his previous books, *Extraordinary Awakenings* explores terrain we all tend to walk but not fully recognize, and his gentle, insistent voice draws out the meaning. There is much to learn here, much to awaken to and embrace in order to let go of habits, preconceptions, and fears and become our highest selves."

— **Michael Jawer**, author of *Sensitive Soul*

"Steve Taylor takes a giant step by revealing how traumatic situations and gritty life challenges can catalyze profound awakening experiences. No longer can these be seen as delusions or throw-away stress responses; instead, they clearly belong in the arena of posit~~ive life-transformative episodes~~ that leave the experiencer profoundly chang~~ed~~

A Sourcebook for 1  of
cy
cy

"A moving book that is right for our times. Some people awaken through a blissful encounter with nature or a mystical experience induced by a psychedelic substance. But others awaken through addiction, imprisonment, life-threatening illness, depression, and other dark nights of the soul. Steve Taylor shows that awakening is always an option — even during dire times — and his book can serve as a life raft for those who are caught in challenging circumstances."

— **David Lukoff**, founder and director of the Spiritual Competency Academy

"*Extraordinary Awakenings* is both extraordinary and ordinary: extraordinary because it describes the sudden lifting of suffering and the deliverance into a more luminous, joyful existence; ordinary because every human being is capable of being what Steve Taylor calls a 'shifter.' We can all shift our consciousness. The stories in this book inspired me to continually wake myself up and contribute to a better, kinder, and more peaceful world."

— **Elizabeth Lesser**, cofounder of Omega Institute and author of the *New York Times* bestseller *Broken Open: How Difficult Times Can Help Us Grow*

"Fascinating and inspiring. Offering more than just a compelling account of traumatic circumstances leading to unexpected spiritual awakenings, Steve Taylor also explores their common features and how they can facilitate our own awakening — something we all can benefit from."

— **Peter Russell**, author of *Letting Go of Nothing* and *From Science to God*

"Mind-blowing. A gripping combination of moving personal stories and groundbreaking psychological research, this inspiring book will help you find the gifts in life's greatest challenges. By connecting the study of personal transformation with even bigger questions about our destiny as a species, Steve Taylor makes the leap from psychologist to visionary."

— **Matthew Green**, author of *Aftershock: Fighting War, Surviving Trauma and Finding Peace*

EXTRAORDINARY AWAKENINGS

EXTRAORDINARY AWAKENINGS

*When Trauma Leads
to Transformation*

STEVE TAYLOR

New World Library
Novato, California

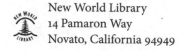

New World Library
14 Pamaron Way
Novato, California 94949

The material in this book is intended for education. It is not meant to take the place of diagnosis and treatment by a qualified medical practitioner or therapist. No expressed or implied guarantee of the effects of the use of the recommendations can be given or liability taken.

Text design by Tona Pearce Myers

Library of Congress Cataloging-in-Publication Data

Names: Taylor, Steve, date, author.
Title: Extraordinary awakenings : when trauma leads to transformation / Steve Taylor.
Description: Novato, California : New World Library, 2021. | Includes bibliographical references and index. | Summary: "A noted psychologist investigates cases of post-traumatic growth, or 'transformation through turmoil,' in which ordinary people from all walks of life undergo a spiritual awakening after a painful experience such as combat, bereavement, addiction, incarceration, life-threatening illness and injury, or severe depression"-- Provided by publisher.
Identifiers: LCCN 2021022375 (print) | LCCN 2021022376 (ebook) | ISBN 9781608687671 (paperback) | ISBN 9781608687688 (epub)
Subjects: LCSH: Suffering--Religious aspects. | Psychic trauma--Religious aspects. | Life change events--Religious aspects. | Religious awakening.
Classification: LCC BL65.S85 T39 2021 (print) | LCC BL65.S85 (ebook) | DDC 204/.42--dc23
LC record available at https://lccn.loc.gov/2021022375
LC ebook record available at https://lccn.loc.gov/2021022376

First printing, September 2021
ISBN 978-1-60868-767-1
Ebook ISBN 978-1-60868-768-8
Printed in Canada on 100% postconsumer-waste recycled paper

 New World Library is proud to be a Gold Certified Environmentally Responsible Publisher. Publisher certification awarded by Green Press Initiative.

10   9   8   7   6   5   4   3   2   1

The deeper that sorrow carves into your being,
the more joy you can contain.

— KAHLIL GIBRAN

CONTENTS

INTRODUCTION

Human life has always involved a great deal of hardship and turmoil. The Buddha was right when he established his first noble truth that "life is suffering" (or, according to some interpretations, that life "involves" suffering). For most of our ancestors, life was an endless cycle of various forms of suffering — the physical suffering of hunger, illness, and warfare; the social suffering of oppression and injustice; the psychological suffering of frequent bereavements and lack of freedom and opportunity. For modern human beings who are fortunate enough to live fairly secure and affluent lives — such as many Europeans and North Americans — suffering has become more oriented toward the psychological than the physical. We may not be as prone to poverty, hunger, and illness, but our psychological sufferings are manifold. We suffer the stress of demanding daily lives and competitive societies, along with the mental strain of being bombarded with massive amounts of sensory stimuli and information. We suffer the isolation and alienation of fragmented urban lifestyles that lack a sense of community. We suffer depression due to isolation and a lack of meaning and purpose in our lives.

It is difficult to make sense of human suffering. The idea that there could be anything *positive* about our suffering may seem absurd. But many people find that suffering does have positive effects, at least in the long term. In recent years psychologists have devoted a lot of time to studying the phenomenon of "post-traumatic growth" (PTG). The idea is that different types of trauma — such as bereavement, serious illness, accidents, oppression, and divorce — may ultimately lead to significant personal development. Research has shown that around half of all people experience some form of personal growth after traumatic events. In the long run, they feel a new sense of inner strength and confidence and of gratitude for life and for other people. They develop more intimate and authentic relationships and have a wider perspective, with a clear sense of what is important in life and what isn't.[1]

In this book we will examine another, related phenomenon, which I call "transformation through turmoil" (or TTT).[2] We will investigate the miraculous phenomenon of how intense psychological suffering can bring about a sudden and dramatic shift into a new identity. The book will show you how spiritual awakening can occur in the most unexpected places. You will meet some amazing human beings, all of whom have experienced the worst predicaments that human life can offer but have responded to their suffering not by breaking down but by shifting up to a higher-functioning awakened state, like a phoenix rising from the ashes. You will meet people who woke up following bereavement, after a deep depression that led them to the brink of suicide, after years of addiction that broke them down to nothing, or after an accident or illness led to an intense encounter with their own mortality. You will meet long-term prisoners who experienced transformation as a result of incarceration and soldiers who woke up as a result of the stress and anxiety of warfare.

The Most Remarkable Transformation

Transformation through turmoil is the most remarkable phenomenon I have ever come across. It's amazing that human beings are capable of transforming so suddenly and radically that they feel they are completely different people living in the same body. People who were addicted to drugs or alcohol for many years are suddenly freed of their craving, because they are reborn as new human beings who don't carry any addictions. People who spent years struggling against depression suddenly find the burden of their mental torment lifted, as they transition to a state of permanent ease and well-being. People who attempted suicide begin to see life as a glorious and miraculous adventure. People who have been imprisoned for many years undergo a spiritual liberation that frees them from any sense of restriction or deprivation.

There is a striking uniformity in the state that the "shifters" (as I call people who have undergone this transformation) describe, as if the state were an unfolding level of human potential that everyone may have access to. It is a higher-functioning state in which people live much more easily and effectively than normal. People who have experienced TTT feel a constant sense of well-being and a strong sense of connection to other people, to nature, and to the world as a whole. The world seems a fascinating and beautiful place to them. They are less materialistic and self-centered, more compassionate and altruistic. They have a strong sense of meaning and purpose and an intense sense of gratitude for everything in their lives, and for life itself.

It sounds like a miracle, akin to the born-again experience that followers of some religions describe. It is superficially similar to this — and indeed, we will see a few cases in which people did interpret their shift in religious terms, because this was the only framework they had to understand it. But in reality, TTT is quite a different phenomenon. Born-again religious experiences are usually conceptual experiences in which a person's belief system changes and they adopt a new lifestyle based on those beliefs. But TTT is nonconceptual. If anything, it is about *letting go* of beliefs rather than adopting them. TTT is a complete transformation of identity and being. This is probably why research shows that born-again religious experiences are usually temporary, whereas TTT is invariably permanent.

The Aims of This Book

I have been researching TTT for many years, and I felt it was time to share some of the incredible stories of transformation I have collected along the way. The core chapters of this book deal with specific types of intense suffering — such as combat, incarceration, bereavement, encounters with death, and addiction — and describe spiritual awakenings that have taken place in the midst of them. Although I will occasionally refer to other sources, this book is based on many long and detailed interviews I conducted with people who have experienced "extraordinary awakenings." To a large extent, I allow these shifters to speak in their own words, although I also summarize details of their stories, and I analyze and comment on them.

It was an incredible experience to interview the shifters. I often found myself welling up with tears or having shivers run up and down my spine. It is tremendously moving to hear accounts from people who have been to the furthest extremes of loss and suffering, who have faced the most desperate and desolate predicaments that human beings can possibly experience. But even more than that, it is inspiring that these people have risen so gloriously from the depths of their suffering and are now living such fulfilling and purposeful lives. I'm sure that as you read these stories, you will be as powerfully affected as I was.

These stories also illustrate the inspiring resilience of the human spirit. They show that we human beings tend to underestimate ourselves. As we go through our everyday lives, working and socializing and entertaining ourselves, we usually only scratch the surface of our potential. All the while, there are vast, deep reserves of strength and skill and resilience inside us that we are unaware of. We may lack self-confidence and self-esteem, thinking of ourselves as inept or weak. But when we are severely tested by life, we find that we have the inner strength to deal with almost any challenge that comes our way.

At the same time, these experiences illustrate how *limited* our normal human state is. The term *awakening* implies that we are normally in a state of sleep. And this is what everyone who experiences TTT discovers: that what we think of as normal is an aberrational state that creates psychological suffering and presents us with a false vision of reality. Awakening gives us access to a fuller, higher-functioning state in which life seems easy and we feel at home in the world.

Along with sharing the incredible stories of the shifters, later in the book I look into the *meaning* of these experiences. Is it possible to explain them? What psychological factors lie behind them? Why do they happen to some people and not others? We will see that, although TTT is certainly miraculous, it is not wholly mysterious; in fact, it can largely be explained in psychological terms. As such, the phenomenon has much to teach us about the process of spiritual awakening.

This brings us to another important aspect of the book. In the final chapter we will see that TTT can offer us some valuable principles that we can apply to our own spiritual development. This includes releasing our psychological attachments, facing and contemplating our mortality, and responding to suffering with an attitude of acknowledgment and acceptance.

With their more positive and meaningful lives, the shifters offer us a glimpse of a new kind of future for the human race, and a new kind of world, free from the brutality and madness that presently afflict us. Indeed, as we will discuss further on, there is an evolutionary aspect to extraordinary awakenings. They show us what the human race could be, and even what we may *inevitably* be, at some point in the future.

The Meaning of *Extraordinary*

In the title of this book, the word *extraordinary* has two meanings. On the one hand, it refers to the extraordinary circumstances in which TTT occurs. These circumstances, such as combat or incarceration, are extraordinary in the sense that we might not normally associate them with spiritual awakening. They are also extraordinary in that they involve a huge amount of deprivation and loss and a level of despair that seems to be the polar opposite of the bliss and harmony of spiritual awakening. This applies to situations such as bereavement and addiction.

However, the term *extraordinary* also applies to the nature of the experiences the shifters undergo. Their experiences are extraordinary in the sense that, as mentioned above, they are miraculous. Some of them seem to defy rationality, as in the cases of addicts who undergo a sudden identity shift for no apparent reason and in the process become permanently free of craving. This also applies to some astounding near-death experiences in which people feel that they have encountered an ultimate reality of light and love and sometimes encounter supernatural beings.

I want to point out that I have been selective in the experiences I have focused on. There are some types of psychological turmoil and trauma that I could easily have based whole chapters on but have omitted for reasons of space. If I had covered every type of psychological turmoil, the book would be at least twice the length. I considered a chapter on TTT in new mothers, who undergo a transformation due to the stress and sleeplessness of having a new baby. (In *The Leap*, I told the story of Marita, who experienced post-natal depression after the birth of her second child and underwent TTT after four nights without sleep.[3]) I also considered a chapter on TTT in refugees. In 2018 I led a research project at my university on the traumatic experiences of asylum seekers and refugees, and found some instances of PTG and TTT in our participants. I also considered a chapter on TTT in people who have become seriously ill or disabled. If I write a sequel to this book, it will certainly include these types of experiences.

It is also important to bear in mind that awakening sometimes occurs in a more ordinary way than I describe in this book. In many cases, spiritual awakening may not be related to psychological turmoil at all. The most common form of spiritual awakening is the gradual kind that occurs through many years of following spiritual practices and paths. In this book I'm not attempting to provide a general overview of the topic of spiritual awakening (I do this in *The Leap*). Rather, I am focusing on a particular type of transformation: the extraordinary awakening that may occur in the midst of extreme human suffering.

1

PEACE IN THE MIDST OF WAR

Transformation on the Battlefield

B efore we begin our investigation, I'd like to define what I mean by "spiritual awakening." The term *spiritual* is often associated with religion, but that's not how I use it. The experiences you'll read about in this book have nothing to do with religion (although they might be interpreted in religious terms by religious people). Spiritual awakening is simply a shift into a more intense and expansive state of awareness. In awakening, it's as if the filters or boundaries that limit normal human awareness fall away. At the same time, awakening is a higher-functioning psychological state — a state of enhanced well-being and freedom from psychological discord, in which people live more authentically and creatively.

We can think of four different areas in which our awareness expands and intensifies in awakening. First, our awareness becomes more intense in a *perceptual* sense. The world around us becomes more vivid and alive. We notice things we didn't pay attention to before. Things that used to seem mundane and boring now seem beautiful and fascinating. We become more sensitive to the joys of music and art and the grandeur of natural landscapes or beautiful buildings.

Our awareness also intensifies *inwardly*. We become aware of an increased depth and richness within our own being. We realize that there is more to our own consciousness, and our own identity, than we previously suspected. You could compare this to a diver swimming in shallow water and then passing through an underwater tunnel and suddenly finding a vast ocean stretching beneath.

In addition, our awareness intensifies in terms of our *connection* to others, and to the world in general. We become more empathic toward other people, other living beings, and the whole of the natural world. We feel more love and compassion for others. We feel that we're not just individuals but part of a wider network of being, sharing consciousness rather than just possessing it. We feel connected to nature and so feel a new sense of respect and responsibility for it.

Finally, our awareness expands or intensifies in a *conceptual* sense, giving us a wider and more global vision of the world. We transcend the self-centered perspective in which our personal concerns seem more important than anything else. We develop a much wider sense of perspective, with a greater concern for other people's problems and for social and global issues. In the normal human state, we tend to cling to group identities, through nationality, religion, or politics. We see members of other groups as different from us and may withhold empathy and respect from them. But in awakening, we move beyond group identity. If we identity with anything, it is with the human race as a whole, without any distinctions. We feel equally respectful of and empathic toward all human beings, no matter how different they may superficially seem. (You can refer to the appendix of this book for a full list of the main characteristics of wakefulness.)

Awakening can also occur in a *temporary* form. Awakening *experiences* are brief glimpses of wakefulness that can last anywhere from a few seconds to a few hours — perhaps even a few days. In these moments, our awareness expands and intensifies in all the ways I've described above. Our perception becomes more intense and vivid, our inner life becomes more expansive, we feel a powerful sense of connection with other people and with the natural world, and so on. In intense awakening experiences, we may feel as if we are lifted out of ourselves, into oneness with all things. We may become aware of a dynamic spiritual force — whose nature is bliss or love — that pervades all things and all space. However, after a certain amount of time, our normal psychological structures reestablish themselves, and we lose this heightened awareness — or, you could say, we fall back to sleep.

For many people, awakening experiences are the beginning of a spiritual journey. After their first glimpse of wakefulness, they feel drawn to spiritual paths and practices as a way of returning to the more intense and expansive state they experienced. As a result, they may gradually cultivate an ongoing state of wakefulness.

Although the main focus of this book is permanent transformation, we will look at some temporary awakening experiences too, in passing. In fact, we will begin our investigation by looking at a temporary awakening experience that eventually led to an ongoing state of wakefulness.

"I Was in a Moment That Seemed Eternal" – Gus's Story

The Falkland Islands are a group of islands in the Pacific Ocean, about three hundred miles off the east coast of South America. They were discovered and colonized by Europeans and claimed by Britain in 1830. Ever since, they have been occupied by English-speaking peoples. However, Argentina has always claimed sovereignty of the islands, and in 1982, they launched an invasion. This led to a war with Great Britain, which lasted ten weeks and cost more than nine hundred lives. It ended with Britain retaining sovereignty.

Gus Hales was one of the 26,000 British soldiers who were sent over to defend the islands. One day, while waiting for orders to advance on the battlefield, he had a life-changing experience:

Life becomes very intense before a battle. You're forced to live in the moment. I remember sitting there thinking, "I don't want to die." I wanted to go home. I wanted to run away. I contemplated feigning injury. Internally there was all this resistance, all this internal dialogue saying, "Why am I doing this? I don't want to do this." I was thinking of how I was going to die and remember telling myself that I wanted to be taken out quickly. I realized how tenuous life is, how fickle and fragile. This could be the night that everything ended.

And there came a point when I just felt, "Fuck it — if I'm going to die, I'm going to die." I let go. I reconciled myself with the thought of death, and there was peace. Complete peace. For a couple of hours there was no future or past. Time disappeared, and I was filled with ecstasy. I was in a moment that seemed eternal. I realized that there was nothing to fear. Everything was okay. I realized that my life didn't mean very much — I didn't know how much longer I was going to own it. I was completely reconciled to whatever happened.

After the war, like many soldiers, Gus suffered from posttraumatic stress disorder (PTSD) for several years. He felt full of anxiety and anger, and had terrible nightmares, but couldn't explain his feelings to anyone. However, he never forgot his timeless experience on the battlefield and longed to return to that state. Sometimes he used to sit up all night in bed, "trying to get back to that timeless moment when everything was okay. It was a kind of vigil, like I was meditating before I knew what meditation was."

After years of suffering, Gus was referred to a psychiatric clinic that treated veterans with PTSD. Another veteran gave him a book about Buddhism, and he was intrigued by the idea that it was possible to control his thoughts and change his attitude toward them. He visited a Buddhist monastery, where he heard a monk say that suffering comes from attachment. He realized that this explained what had happened to him before the battle — he had given up his attachment to life. Gus then had a personal meeting with a monk who was also an ex-soldier. This meeting was pivotal for Gus:

I thought he would be interested in my story. I thought I was someone special – I was an ex-paratrooper, I'd fought in the Falklands War. But he had no interest in my story whatsoever. He said, "So what do you want to talk about?" I told him that the war was in my mind all the time, that I couldn't stop thinking about my experiences in the Falklands. And he just said, in quite a dismissive way, "Oh, don't worry about them – they're just thoughts." Then he walked out.

Shortly afterward I went to a meditation group, and at first I couldn't meditate. My mind was too busy. But there was a brief moment that took me back to my experience before the battle, when everything was still. It was just a few seconds, but I thought, if I've done it for five seconds, why can't I do it for ten seconds, or a minute, or longer?

I realized that I was keeping my pain alive in my thoughts. The war had ended ten years earlier, but in my mind I was still fighting it. I realized that my suffering didn't come from the war but from my internal dialogue about the war – what if I'd done this, what if I'd done that, asking questions that could never be answered. The pain came from holding on to all that.

Encouraged by his experience of liberation while meditating, Gus enrolled in a ten-day Vipassana meditation retreat. He found that the rigid discipline and structure of the retreat appealed to his soldier's mentality. He cultivated the ability to rest in the present, observing his thoughts and feelings. He sensed more and more space opening up between his thoughts, until gradually his PTSD symptoms began to ebb. As he told me, "Meditation taught me that you can leave thoughts alone. You don't have to follow them but just be aware and observe what you are thinking. The same with sensations of anxiety and fear. If you observe and don't react, they fade away."

Knowing how common PTSD was among his fellow veterans, Gus was determined to share his discovery. He became a Buddhist, and over the years has taught meditation to many veterans and led many Vipassana retreats of his own. In addition, he has campaigned to raise awareness of the mental health issues of veterans, including their high rates of homelessness and suicide. In 2018–2019, he went on hunger strike twice to bring attention to the issue, hoping for more support from the UK government. As he said to me, "I want to help people, to try to relieve their suffering. The ability to be present has transformed my life, so I want to share my insight. I used to think of it as a goal: 'I've got to get enlightenment!' But then I realized that it's not about gaining something — enlightenment is all about what you lose, what you let go of."

The Paradox of War

Nothing illustrates the evil aspects of human nature more than warfare: the practice of fighting, killing, and conquering other groups of human beings. Along with being heinous in and of itself, warfare often allows a whole host of other evil practices to rear their heads, such as rape, torture, theft, and slavery. Warfare seems to offer proof that human beings are brutal savages whose evil nature is camouflaged by a thin veneer of civilization.

Anthropologists used to think that human groups have always fought wars, but many now believe that warfare is actually quite a late development in human history. As I discussed in my book *The Fall*, prehistoric human beings were actually fairly peaceful. War didn't become endemic to human societies until about six thousand years ago. Even then, it was largely confined to certain parts of the world — mainly the Middle East and Central Asia. But over the following millennia, it spread over most of the globe.

Since then, human history has been, as the psychologist and philosopher William James put it, "a bath of blood."[1] The peak of war madness was probably from the nineteenth century to the mid-twentieth century. During this time, European countries were almost constantly at war with one another. Between 1740 and 1897, there were 230 wars and revolutions in Europe, and some countries were almost bankrupting themselves with their military expenditure. After this came our planet's first two truly international conflicts, during which around a hundred million people were killed.

How is it possible that such brutality could be associated with awakening experiences or spiritual transformation? Surely spirituality belongs to the highest aspects of human nature, while war belongs to the lowest. Spirituality is the realm of saints; war is the realm of psychopaths.

All this is true, of course. Yet my research has shown that intense psychological turmoil is a major trigger of both temporary awakening experiences and permanent awakenings. War is certainly a powerful source of psychological turmoil, so we shouldn't be surprised that in the midst of so much bleakness and brutality, the light of the spirit sometimes breaks through. Transformation through turmoil shows that seemingly contradictory states like despair and joy or chaos and peace are not binary opposites. They are symbiotically related. And this is certainly true of warfare.

Awakening Experiences in Combat

In my research I have found that the kind of temporary awakening experience that Gus had before his battle is not uncommon. Not long after the publication of my study of awakening experiences in 2010, *Waking from Sleep*, a woman named Phyllis wrote to me, telling me about an awakening experience she had while serving in Afghanistan, on her third deployment with the Army National Guard. She was living in a tent on Bagram Airfield, in a state of constant stress and danger. Air attacks on the airfield took place every day. Sirens would sound, and she and the other soldiers would run to a nearby bunker to take shelter. And one day, she had an experience similar to Gus's:

A wave of something I can only describe as "super happiness" washed over me, and I ceased having any feelings of worry or fear. I was just super calm and incredibly attuned to feelings of happiness. It didn't matter about life or death anymore – even during the usually nerve-rattling "incoming!" sirens. It lasted about five hours and then gradually dimmed to a peacefulness that kept me going until we arrived back in the States, about seven days later.

Phyllis didn't understand the experience. She wanted to tell the other members of her squad about it but had no idea how to interpret or explain it. As with Gus, it was only years later, when she learned about spirituality, that she began to make sense of her experience.

An even more powerful example of an awakening experience was sent to me by a Vietnam veteran (we'll call him Ted, since he is a private person and asked me not to reveal his identity). It happened in 1968, when his combat base came under heavy attack, with major casualties, and he was sure that he was going to die too:

At one point, after carrying yet another severely wounded marine to a waiting chopper, something happened to me. I came out of myself. I expanded infinitely. I disappeared. It didn't last long, but it was the most powerful experience I've ever had. From that moment my anxiety disappeared and I knew that everything was all right, no matter if I lived or died. Words escape me. There was no "me" there to comprehend the "awakening experience," so how can I describe it? The Battle of Khe Sanh lasted seventy-seven days. I felt peaceful for the remainder of the battle. I was not wounded in those seventy-seven days, although more than twenty-five hundred marines were wounded and more than eight hundred killed.

Ted returned from Vietnam in 1969, and like a lot of vets, he drank to try to forget the trauma of war. Because he couldn't make sense of his awakening experience, he repressed it and then forgot about it. But five years later, a friend who was concerned for his well-being persuaded him to attend a Buddhist meditation group. During the meditation, his experience on the battlefield came back to him as a powerful recollection. From that point on, he became a spiritual seeker. He realized that meditation and spirituality could help him recapture his awakening experience. Ted sensed that his experience was essentially "a state of living in the present and the acceptance of anything that comes, no matter how brutal." And he knew that he could cultivate presence and acceptance through meditation.

Unfortunately, Ted has never managed to replicate his experience on the battlefield. As he told me, "I've spent the past fifty or so years trying without success to replicate that experience. Nothing has come close to my awakening experience at Khe Sanh." But rather than feeling frustrated, Ted told me, "The memory alone of the intense, transformative experience is enough to sustain me. It has played a major role in everything I've done since."

Ted's story recalls the experiences of a German soldier, a young aristocrat named Karlfried Graf Dürckheim, during the First World War. Dürckheim's countless encounters with death during the war — witnessing the deaths of others and almost dying many times himself — brought him into contact with a deeper aspect of his own being, an essence that he sensed was *beyond* death. As he said, in a conversation with the Indian guru Swami Prabhupada, "When death was near and you had accepted death...then you realized something which has nothing to do whatsoever with death.... So this marked me very much. It was the very beginning of my inner way."[2] After the war, like Ted, Dürckheim became a spiritual seeker. He gave up his property and inheritance and began to study Eastern spiritual texts. He eventually traveled to Japan, where he studied Zen Buddhism for several years, and was one of the first people to introduce Zen teachings to the West.[3]

PTG and Permanent Transformation

Although they are temporary, awakening experiences almost always change people in a significant way, as the stories of Gus, Phyllis, and Ted illustrate. The experiences might only last for a few seconds, a few minutes, or a few hours, but people often refer to them as the most important events of their lives. People usually become more optimistic and trusting in life, with an increased sense of meaning and purpose. Like Ted, people treasure the memory of the experience, which has a calming and consoling effect. Most notably, awakening experiences usually turn people into spiritual seekers.

Nevertheless, there is a big difference between having an awakening experience and actually *becoming* awakened. It is like the difference between briefly visiting a beautiful landscape and actually *living* in that landscape. A brief visit to a landscape can be inspiring and can change your outlook to some degree. It makes you realize that your home environment is not the whole world, that the world is larger and more beautiful than you assumed. You have the hope of one day returning to the landscape, and start to explore the possibility of traveling back there. But a person who attains permanent wakefulness transforms in a deep-rooted and all-encompassing way.[4]

Permanent awakening is certainly not uncommon among veterans. This is indicated by research showing that, in addition to causing high levels of PTSD, combat can also lead to significant levels of post-traumatic growth (PTG). A 2006 study of veterans of the Persian Gulf found numerous cases of PTG. It was especially pronounced in veterans who had faced intense life-threatening situations and who now felt an enhanced sense of appreciation. Like Dürckheim, after coming close to death, they felt intensely grateful just to be alive.[5] A 2010 study of American veterans of both the Iraq and Afghanistan wars found that the more combat they were exposed to, the more likely they were to experience PTG.[6] PTG is sometimes divided into five areas: appreciation of life, relationships with others, new possibilities in life, personal strength, and spiritual change. In the above study, 72 percent of the veterans reported significant growth in at least one of these areas.

The difference between PTG and transformation through turmoil (TTT) is really one of degree. Particularly when it occurs gradually (as in Gus's case), TTT can be seen as an intense form of PTG. Conversely, a normal degree of PTG could be seen as a less intense form of spiritual awakening.

I described one amazing example of permanent spiritual awakening through the trauma of warfare in *Out of the Darkness*, that of my friend and mentor Russel Williams, who experienced a powerful spiritual awakening in 1950 at the age of twenty-nine. It was precipitated by many years of suffering and trauma, particularly during the Second World War. Russel was in London during the Blitz, when German airplanes pounded the city with bombs night after night for weeks on end. He came close to death several times, including a classic near-death experience after he was electrocuted and suddenly found himself out in space, looking down on his body. Most traumatically, he took part in the evacuation of Dunkirk, helping to ferry stranded and wounded soldiers across the English Channel as the German army was approaching.

It is well known that many of the soldiers at Dunkirk suffered PTSD (or combat stress reaction, as the British referred to it at that time), and Russel was no exception. His experience at Dunkirk was the only thing that he never talked about in detail — it was too painful, he said. He said only that the horror was impossible to describe and that it illustrated both the best and worst in human nature.

At the end of the war, Russel felt broken down and disoriented. After some wanderings, he took a job at a traveling circus, where he looked after horses, grooming and feeding them. He came to feel a powerful sense of connection with the horses and later realized that this life of service was a spiritual practice for him. As he became more connected to the horses, observing them more and more closely, his mind became quiet. And this led to a sudden spiritual awakening. He woke up one morning and realized that he no longer had a sense of separation from animals and human beings, that his mind was quiet, and that his anxiety and discontent had disappeared, leaving a feeling of deep inner peace. (See Russel's book *Not I, Not Other Than I* for more details.)

"It Was Just Me and Something Bigger" — Gary's Story

At the university where I teach, we have a master's degree called Interdisciplinary Psychology. The name is a little misleading — a more appropriate name would perhaps be Spiritual Psychology or Alternative Psychology. It's a joy to teach the course, partly because it's so close to my own interests (and because I have had the freedom to develop some of the course content) but mainly because of the wonderful students we attract. These include a large portion of mature students, aged thirty or over, who have had spiritual experiences or full-fledged spiritual awakenings. They enroll in the course because they want to explore their experiences, to find out why they occurred, and to see how common they are. Perhaps most of all, they are trying to find a different view of reality to make sense of their experiences — an alternative to mainstream materialism, which sees human beings as biological machines and views spiritual experiences as illusions. They are also sometimes eager to study spiritual ideas from an academic perspective so that they can promote them and make them more acceptable in mainstream culture.

In recent years, we have had two British ex-soldiers in the course. In 2016 a well-built and serious-minded man named Gary (not his real name), thirty-two years old, joined the course. Since he was fairly quiet in class, it was a while before I realized that Gary was an ex-soldier who had had some remarkable experiences. During a session on awakening experiences, I split the class into small groups, asking them to describe their experiences to one another. I overheard Gary describing an experience he'd had in Iraq when he was serving in the British army in 2009, during the Second Gulf War. I later interviewed him about the experience, and about his experiences in general. Like Ted above, Gary found the experience difficult to describe but managed to convey its essence. He was on the battlefield with his unit when a bomb went off close by:

> I was looking around, trying to find the bomb shelters to go and hide in, and I found I could see the whole area incredibly clearly, as if I was above it. I had panoramic vision. I felt like I was out of my body but also still in it. Part of me was out there in space, but part of me was still inside myself. I felt calm and serene, although I could have been killed. I was only scared when I thought about it afterward. At the time I was calm and focused, doing everything I needed to do. Like making sure that other people were okay, looking around, trying to find the bomb shelters. At the time I thought, well, maybe it's just down to adrenaline. But I knew it was more than that. And after doing this course, I know that for sure.

Gary had another powerful experience when he was driving through the desert and his Land Rover crashed:

> The Land Rover spun over eight times, rolling down a hill, and everything went into slow motion. It was like the best roller coaster I've ever been on. There was a sense of total serenity, just being in the driver's seat, spinning around. I didn't normally put on my helmet when I drove the Land Rover, but that day I did, and it saved me. As it crashed down, I went forward and hit my head on the windshield. But again I felt calm and serene. I had this feeling of, well, this is out of my control, I can't do anything about it, so I might as well just enjoy it. There was nothing at all to worry about; it all seemed perfectly fine.

Although he didn't really understand these experiences, Gary felt changed, especially after the Land Rover crash. He felt connected to something bigger than himself, which he felt was also somehow inside him. He had a strong impulse to connect with other people. Although he had always been something of a loner, now he felt a need to be a part of a community. As he told me, "It was me and something bigger. I wasn't in isolation anymore."

Gary began to feel that the life he was leading wasn't suited to him and decided to leave the army. At first he found civilian life difficult to adjust to, but he had a strong sense that everything would work out if he followed his instincts. He had been brought up in an intensely religious family, as a Jehovah's Witness, and although he had left the faith, he started to study religion again, to try to make some sense of his awakening experiences. He reread the Gospels and the Psalms and began to attend Quaker meetings. Then he explored beyond Christianity, attending as many local spiritual groups and meetings as he could, studying Buddhism, Taoism, and yoga. Eventually, this search for understanding led him to our master's degree.

At the time I interviewed Gary, it was six years after he'd left the army, and I sensed that he was still in an integration phase, exploring the meaning of his experiences. But it was clear that he had undergone a powerful positive transformation. He has a deeper understanding of himself and others, is no longer interested in money or possessions, and enjoys just "chilling out" and living in the moment. He now has a much greater appreciation of nature, which seems more real and beautiful than before. He feels that now his main aim in life is "just helping other people. Or just forming bonds with other people." He still feels a sense of connection to something larger than himself, something that is guiding his life and expressing itself through his life. He feels he has "woken up" to a much wider and deeper reality whose existence he never suspected before, as if he had been seeing the world with blinders on before but now had a panoramic view.

"I Stand Back and Watch It All Come and Go" – David's Story

The year before Gary joined the course, we had another ex-soldier student, David. (Their paths didn't cross, as David had left the university before I realized Gary was also a veteran.) David was in the military for twenty-two years and had been in civilian life for only five years when he joined our course. His transformation was so powerful and dramatic that we'll examine it in more detail than any of the other stories in this chapter.

David joined the military partly because his older brothers were already in the army, and it seemed natural to follow in their footsteps. His parents were proud of his brothers, and he wanted them to feel proud of him too, so he joined the Royal Air Force. Just a few months later, the First Gulf War broke out. In January 1991, at the age of eighteen, he was sent to Iraq:

It was an eye-opener. I had never witnessed combat or battle or death. But now I started having to clear bodies. I was working nights. Whenever we were attacked by Scud missiles I would sit outside on the apron [the part of the airport where aircraft are parked], looking up at the clear night sky and the stars, watching missiles fly over. That was the first time I had an experience that I couldn't explain. In fact, I don't think I understood it fully until I did my master's degree. I lay in the sand and looked up at the sky, and my breathing just seemed to regulate itself. I felt like I was floating, high up in the air. I was lifted up, out of myself. The Scud would fly across, and a Patriot missile would fly across, and they would hit each other. People were taking photographs, and I felt like I was up there, in the middle of it, not knowing whether I was going to live or die. There was a feeling of … it was overwhelming. I was close to tears. It was a beautiful experience. I felt like my lungs were huge and I was breathing in the whole world. I couldn't believe how amazing it was, the panoramic view. I couldn't put the experience into words. I certainly couldn't tell any of my friends about it. I felt alone but alive. I couldn't relate it to anything, so I had to push it to one side and move on.

A lot of things happened in the First Gulf War that I never wanted to see. Things like watching people being assassinated in front of me – Iraqi soldiers who were captured by Kuwaiti soldiers at the airport we had taken over. I couldn't do anything about it. It made me aware of the reality of death. It could have been me. That was someone's son, someone's brother, someone's uncle.

Another time I carried ten bodies off a Hercules helicopter, when the Americans accidentally blew one of our tanks up. Ten of our soldiers were killed, with just a couple of survivors. I had to carry the guys in their body bags into the aircraft, knowing that some of them were just seventeen or eighteen years old, the same age as me.

That First Gulf War changed my life. I was out there for five months. It was an experience of realizing that I'm not immortal, that life in its current form isn't meant to last. It had a traumatic effect on me too, of course. Soon after my return I started having nightmares, waking up in cold sweats. I had flashbacks, night terrors. I felt a lot of anger.

After that I did a tour of Northern Ireland in 1992 and spent most of my days flying in helicopters, over the mountains of South Armagh, feeling alive and exhilarated. I had a series of other powerful experiences – unique moments of life and death. One day I saw a Puma helicopter and a Gazelle helicopter collide, killing all the people onboard the Puma. It was another experience of the fragility of life and of losing people I worked with. Other people were shot by snipers or were caught in an ambush and killed.

It made me feel that my life was important. I started living my life to the full as a way to honor my friends who had died. They can't live their lives anymore, but I still can. I started to enjoy and embrace moments of solitude. I started to take everything in, to experience the moment – sights, smells, sounds. I started to really appreciate the present. I started to do breathing exercises, paying attention to the breath going in and out, the pattern of breathing. I loved the feeling of weightlessness. I had no idea that it was a kind of meditation.

I started to annoy some people because I became very relaxed. They would get anxious, and I'd tell them not to worry.

People used to tell me I was too laid-back. People just didn't get me. And that still happens now. But it's because of my experiences that I'm so relaxed – because I have a sense of what's really important. It's given me a full-on sense of perspective. In the moment we live in, what is there to be fearful of or to regret? We're always just here.

A few years later, I went to the desert again, for the Second Gulf War. I was on a special operation in Iraq. I would lay in the sand, just looking up at the stars, which were amazing. There was a time when we had to go ashore with the Navy Seals and the Royal Marines assault teams in preparation for a big assault on Baghdad. It was the first time I saw St. Elmo's fire. The Chinooks flew over the desert, and when they were low enough, it created a dust cloud. Because sand is effectively glass, when it hits the rotor blades, the blades light up. So I was sitting on the sand while the helicopter was hovering, and there were two massive bright lights in the sky, like angel wings, so close I felt I could touch them. It was so beautiful. People thought I was strange, sitting there and gazing. I didn't feel like a human being. I didn't feel separate from space and time. It all merged into one thing.

When the Chinook lifted off with a load underneath, all of a sudden there was nothing. Pure stillness. It felt so still and beautiful that I didn't want to breathe. I thought I would ruin the stillness by breathing. It was an unreal feeling, listening to the stillness. It was almost as if I were dead. It was an overwhelming feeling.

But the Second Gulf War was far worse. We had to go to the Al-Faw Peninsula, in the southeast of Iraq, where the oil fields were. The Iraqis had set fire to the oil fields in the First Gulf War, and we had to protect the fields, to make sure they weren't burned again. It was my job, with my team, to make sure that the Chinooks had a safe landing area and that the mortar platoon could get all the equipment in, to set up the mortar field, before the battle began.

We had to go from our ship, the HMS *Ark Royal*, on to flat-bottomed boats, and sail to a place called Red Beach. When we arrived at the peninsula, we had to take down the telegraph poles so a metal road could be used as a landing site for the

Chinooks, to drop off the troops and for all the equipment that was needed for the battle.

After we had done that, I was waiting in a trench. We knew where the enemy were, and a message went out to them, saying that we didn't want to fight, that we would rather they gave up their arms without a battle. But they wanted to fight. So unfortunately, the Americans sent in gunships and helicopters and started firing on the enemy lines. From about three o'clock in the morning, I was sitting in my trench listening to the screams of the Iraqi soldiers.

At first light we made our way over to the enemy trenches, and I found an Iraqi soldier who had lost his limbs and was obviously close to death. There was nothing I could do for him — he was losing blood everywhere. I sat down with him. People were saying, "Why are you sitting with him? He's the enemy." I said, "The guy's dying. He's a human being." "Well, just put him out of his misery and move one." "I can't," I said. "He's a human being."

I was absolutely shocked and devastated, but I wanted to sit with him while he took his last breath. I put my hand on his shoulder and wiped his tears away, as a fellow human being, looking into his eyes. I told him, "I'm with you. It's going to be okay — just close your eyes." I thought the same as I did in the First Gulf War: *This is someone's son, someone's brother. What makes his life worth any less than mine?* It was a powerful spiritual moment that has always stayed with me. I can still see the guy's face now. It doesn't haunt me, but I carry it with me.

All these experiences made me feel like I was making contact with my real self. I felt like, when I joined the forces, I was being the false self that everyone wanted me to be. I felt that now, more and more, I was discovering who I really was. It didn't feel authentic for me to be a soldier.

Those moments shocked me to my core. My feelings were all negative. I didn't want to be in Iraq. I didn't agree with the war. I just wanted to be home. And the next day my back went out. I couldn't stand up. I was in agony. The Americans told me I had a herniated disk. They flew me back to the HMS *Ark Royal*, to the med bay, but they couldn't do anything for me. So I was flown back to Iraq, to a field hospital, and then back to England.

And that was the end of my war. In retrospect, I think it was my body's way of saying "enough," that I wasn't meant to be there anymore, that I didn't belong there. I'd never had any problems with my back before.

Once he was fit to return to work, David worked at Heathrow Airport in London as a civilian liaison officer, meeting soldiers who were flying home due to injury or organizing flights for the relatives of wounded soldiers. He found the emotional aspect of the role fulfilling, helping people who were going through trauma. He felt as though he had found his true vocation in a caring profession.

David did one more tour of duty, in Afghanistan, where he was stung by a camel spider. He developed sepsis, which attacked his internal organs and left him with permanent damage. He developed type 1 diabetes, his thyroid gland stopped working, and he had permanent nerve damage in his left leg, with numbness and constant shooting pains (problems that he still has now).

Once he recovered sufficiently, David was determined to follow his new vocation and trained as a counselor. While still officially in the army, he did a full-time counseling degree before being fully discharged in 2011. While studying, he heard about Eckhart Tolle's books. He took *The Power of Now* with him on a family vacation to Spain, and the book had a revelatory impact:

It was like alarm bells going off. It made so much sense to me. I finally thought: *someone understands what I've been feeling all these years!* All I did on holiday was read sections of the book and put it down and do the exercises it recommends, the mindfulness exercises. I took in all the sights and sounds, the smells, my feelings, my thoughts. I processed everything. It was the best holiday I'd ever had.

The book changed my life. There was a shift in me. All my

anger left me. I didn't realize how much anger I'd been carrying. I didn't realize how toxic the anger had become. I was angry because of the injustice of war, because my friends had died, and because I'd seen other people die in cold blood. The anger had become part of me.

But when I came back from Spain I suddenly thought, *Hold on – where's my anger gone?* It was as if part of me was missing. I had identified with the anger so much it was almost as if I had lost a part of myself. I even missed it a little at first. People were saying to me, "Are you okay? You don't seem like your normal self." I felt lighter, I felt great, but it was difficult to get used to.

David became a university lecturer, then a course leader, and now works for the UK National Health Service as a counselor and psychotherapist. He still has physical issues, including ongoing pain, but says, "Pain has just become natural and normal. I don't take painkillers anymore. It doesn't bother me." He used to have nightmares and would dread going to sleep, until he realized that he could use his dreams positively, as a way of going back in time to good memories. Now he dreams lucidly, aware of his dreams and able to control them. As a result, he now looks forward to going to sleep.

David summarized the transformation he has undergone through his years of military service as follows:

I'm ever so calm. I have a sense of trust and authenticity and love being on my own. I don't take anything for granted. I value life, and I value other people. Wherever I am and whatever I'm doing, I fully experience it. I used to be immersed in my thoughts. I used to be immersed in my anger. Now I stand back and watch it all come and go. Anger's here and anger's gone.

I'm thankful for all the experiences I've been through. I don't regret anything I've ever done. If I've learned from it, it's a valuable experience. All the negative experiences I've had and all the moments of clarity and awareness and awakening and being in the moment – it's all replenished me and made me stronger emotionally.

The purpose of my life is to be here for others, to help them grow and see their own importance. I care so much about other people. That's why I'm alive.

Beyond War

It's difficult to know exactly how common spiritual experiences are among soldiers and veterans. To date, no one has done a systematic study on the topic. (I hope to do so at some point.) However, based on my anecdotal evidence — and the number of examples of such experiences that have come to me so easily — I wouldn't be at all surprised if a significant proportion of all veterans have experienced wakefulness (either temporarily or permanently) as a result of their exposure to combat.

I've met some people who feel an instinctive antipathy to soldiers and anything to do with the army or military. Why should we feel sympathy for soldiers? Their job is to kill other human beings. They are trained to use weapons in order to kill and conquer. They are instruments of the evil military-industrial complex, whose hunger for power and destruction is leading the human race to extinction.

However, we should remember that, for much of human history, people did not become soldiers by choice. Most soldiers were conscripted against their will, forced to fight by governments, kings, or landowners. And even many of those who voluntarily join the army do so because of a lack of other options or due to naive notions of service, glory, and patriotism (of which they are usually soon disavowed).

I find it comforting to think that, throughout the countless wars that human beings have fought, there have surely been millions of people like Gus, Phyllis, Ted, Gary, and David who had glimpses of awakening or underwent permanent transformation. Out of all our ancestors who fought in wars, suffering incredible deprivation and pain and loss, a portion of them must have risen above their suffering to experience moments of ecstasy and freedom. And out of the millions who survived and returned home, some of them must have emerged permanently and positively transformed, to spend the rest of their lives in a higher-functioning, wakeful state.

Warfare is a horrific product of human beings' normal state of "sleep." As I showed in *The Fall*, war is the result of an intensified sense of ego, which causes a lack of empathy for others, a desire to gain wealth and status, and a need for group identity. Warfare arises out of a combination of these factors. At the same time, it is the result of elite groups of psychopaths who hold power over the majority of people, forcing them to further their demented aims and using propaganda to help distort public opinion in their favor.

In this way, nothing is further away from spirituality than warfare. After all, spirituality arises from transcending the intensified sense of ego. Once we transcend the ego, the conditions that give rise to warfare dissolve away. We feel empathy and compassion for others rather than enmity. We feel a sense of wholeness and well-being, which transcends the impulse to gain power and wealth and the need for group identity.

As long as the majority of human beings are asleep, war will always exist. And conversely, our species' only hope of attaining global peace is for the majority of human beings to undergo some degree of spiritual awakening.

And it seems somehow fitting that an activity so strongly associated with sleep holds so much potential to wake us up.

We began this chapter with the story of Gus, who fought in the Falklands War in 1982 and eventually became a Buddhist. In 2007 Gus was part of a group of 250 veterans who returned to the Falklands for a weeklong pilgrimage and a Remembrance Day service. While

there, he separated from the main group and climbed Mount Long-
don, where some of the worst fighting took place.

At the summit of the mountain was a natural shelter among the
granite rocks. A large metal cross had been placed there, along with
some smaller wooden crosses and some photographs of young soldiers who had died there. Gus had brought a small brass statue of
the Buddha with him from England that had been given to him by
the monks at the monastery years earlier. He placed the statue in a
small niche in the rocks as a symbol of both inner and outer peace.
As he put it, he wanted "to put a symbol there, to show other veterans that it had worked for me and could help them too."

2

FREEDOM IN PRISON, PART ONE

Transformation through Incarceration

All our experiences have some degree of spiritual potential. That is, they all have some capacity to bring about awakening experiences, or even to trigger a state of permanent wakefulness. But some experiences have more spiritual potential than others. For example, contact with nature and meditation have a high degree of spiritual potential, whereas shopping and watching television have a low degree. (If you've had an awakening experience while shopping or watching TV, let me know!)

Suffering and turmoil generally have a high degree of spiritual potential, which is why they give rise to the extraordinary awakenings discussed in this book. And some of the types of suffering we're going to examine — such as encountering death, bereavement, and addiction — have an especially high degree of spiritual potential. But in my view, the type of suffering that arguably has the *highest* degree of spiritual potential is incarceration.

In fact, the relationship between incarceration and awakening is such a rich one — with so many examples of prisoners who have had temporary awakening experiences or undergone permanent transformation — that it's impossible to cover it in a single chapter.

So I've divided my examination of the topic into two. The first one covers historical examples of prisoners who have undergone transformation, focusing on prisoners of war and political prisoners. The second (chapter 3 of this book) focuses on contemporary examples of prisoners who have undergone transformation, based on interviews I've conducted for my research.

In part, there is such a strong relationship between incarceration and awakening simply because being imprisoned is an experience of intense suffering. That's why societies have always used imprisonment as a punishment. To be deprived of our liberty and autonomy and denied contact with our family and friends is one of the most painful experiences we can undergo. However, despite the suffering, certain aspects of incarceration make it an especially fertile environment for spiritual awakening.

Voluntary Incarceration

Imagine you have to spend almost all your time in a single room. Even worse, in the short periods when you're allowed out of your room, you can't venture beyond a small, confined area. You are also forced to live without possessions (aside from the bare minimum) and are unable to pursue any career or ambitions. You aren't allowed any autonomy and have to live according to a strict discipline, following preordained rules.

A person might consciously choose to live this kind of life by becoming a monk or nun. Or they might be forced to live this kind of life by being sent to prison.

Some monks effectively live as prisoners. Carthusian monks live in tiny cells (even the word is the same as in a prison!), where they spend most of their time alone and in silence, without any contact with the outside world. They emerge from their cells three times a day, when they come together to pray at church, although even then they're not allowed to speak to each other. They are only allowed to speak twice a week, once on Sundays after lunch and once on Mondays during a communal walk. They don't do any manual work and have no contact with the outside world.

Of course, there are some massive differences between the lives of prisoners and monks or nuns. Choosing to live a restricted life of solitude and detachment is itself an act of freedom, compared to having a restricted life imposed on you as a punishment. Monks also know that they are free to leave the monastic lifestyle and return to the everyday world whenever they wish. And obviously, as environments, prisons and monasteries are vastly different — the former is full of noise, stress, brutality, and psychological discord, while the latter is full of silence and spiritual harmony.

Nevertheless, there are some significant ways in which the life of a long-term prisoner resembles the life of a monk or nun. Specifically, there are two main ways — which are also the two main reasons both ways of life have a high degree of spiritual potential.

First, both are lives of extreme detachment. The attachments that most people normally depend on to provide a sense of identity and security are taken away. For both prisoners and monks, there are no ambitions or hopes for the future. They can't derive identity from a job or profession, or from roles as spouses or parents. They can't build up success or status or collect achievements and material wealth.

In normal life, such attachments are the building blocks of the ego. They make us feel that we are "someone" — important people who feel confident and secure as we go about our lives. Without the attachments, we may feel timid and unsure of ourselves and overwhelmed by the world. But with the attachments in place, we have a strong ego with which to face the world. When these attachments are taken away from us, or when they break down, it is usually a very painful experience. We often feel a terrible sense of loss, failure, and disillusionment. In fact, this is one of the reasons why imprisonment is used so widely as a punishment — because it takes all our attachments away for us, with all the pain and loss that this entails.

But as the voluntary detachment of monks shows, the loss of attachments also holds a lot of spiritual potential. In fact, we will see throughout this book that the miraculous spiritual transformations that occur in the midst of intense suffering are largely due to the breakdown of psychological attachments. (I will explain this in more detail toward the end of the book.)

The second way in which the life of a prisoner resembles the life of a monk is that they both contain a great deal of solitude and inactivity, with a lack of external stimulation. Monks consciously choose quietness and solitude so that they can cultivate their spirituality without any distractions. Most prisoners find solitude and inactivity difficult to cope with. The lack of stimulation creates boredom and frustration and often leads to depression and aggression. But for a small number of prisoners, the lack of distractions may have a positive spiritual effect. It may lead them to reflect on their lives and to explore their being in a way they have never done before. And through doing this, they may encounter a spiritual aspect of their being that was previously hidden.

Over this chapter and the next, we will see how both these factors — along with the general psychological turmoil that any state of suffering generates — give rise to transformation in prisoners.

Prisoners of War

Following from the previous chapter, let's begin by looking at prisoners of war. When soldiers are captured and incarcerated by their enemies, they are usually in an even worse predicament than prisoners who serve sentences after being convicted of crimes. They usually suffer a more extreme level of deprivation, with a near-starvation diet, terrible living conditions, and cruelty at the hands of their captors. In addition, their future is uncertain, with the very real possibility that they may not survive. Along with the other terrible aspects of imprisonment, they have to face the prospect of death.

Research has found high levels of post-traumatic growth among ex-prisoners of war. A 1980 study of American aviators who were captured and incarcerated during the Vietnam War found that many of them felt they had benefited psychologically from the experience. The harsher their experiences, the greater the benefits.[1] Similarly, a study of Israeli veterans of the 1973 Yom Kippur War found that prisoners of war had higher levels of PTG than other soldiers.[2]

Full-fledged spiritual transformation is also not uncommon among prisoners of war. One example is a Scottish soldier named Bill Murray. Soon after the outbreak of the Second World War, Murray was sent to North Africa, where he was captured by German soldiers in 1942. He spent the three remaining years of the war in prison camps. Before the war he had been a keen climber in the Scottish Highlands and decided to spend his empty hours in the camp secretly writing a book about his adventures on the camp's coarse toilet paper. The act of reliving all his climbs, step-by-step, and describing them in writing lifted him above the deprivation and suffering of the prison camps. As he put it, "I learned from sheer necessity to live in the mind rather than the body."[3] Unfortunately, just as the book was nearing completion, he was moved to a different prison camp. He hid the wads of toilet paper in his coat, but they were discovered and confiscated, and he never saw them again.

There was a library at the new camp, and although he was depressed by the loss of his book, Murray devoted himself to reading, particularly psychology and philosophy. One morning a young British officer came up to him in the compound and said, "I've seen you around the last day or two.... It seems you're ready to start on the mystic way. Would you like me to give you instruction?"[4] Murray wasn't sure what he meant by the term *mystic way* but agreed to meet the next day.

Straight after this encounter with the officer, Murray had a powerful awakening experience, which he described in a memoir toward the end of his life:

> I returned straight to my own block feeling a little dazed. As I climbed upstairs to the dormitory, I became aware of an extraordinary sense of joy. It suffused mind and body.…I had stepped out of time into timelessness.…I remember seeing through the windows the barbed-wire fence with its sentry towers, and the prisoners in the compound, all and each transfigured by a beauty that glowed through them, engulfing all as if from another place. Its intensity had a new dimension, so that never afterwards could I bring myself to speak of it, or write down the experience until now, when I know that my life is nearing its end.[5]

Murray had had similar ecstatic experiences when reaching the top of a mountain after a long climb. He had known the feeling of being completely present with an awareness of "a more real world underlying the material." But this was a much more intense experience. As he put it, "I seemed to have entered a timeless 'now' of a much higher degree than before.… This time I came away with a sure knowledge. The eternal world 'is.' Our material world is plainly real too: each inhere in the other: the finite within the infinite. The one embraces both."[6]

When he met the officer the next morning, Murray was introduced to a group of a half dozen soldiers who were following the mystic way. They formed a study group, meeting regularly to discuss spiritual texts and ideas and to practice meditation. Although he had never been aware of spirituality before, Murray recognized that he had had the kind of experience that mystics such as Plotinus and St. John of the Cross described. Despite the physical suffering of the camp, and the uncertainty of his survival, he felt invigorated and elated.

Not long after his awakening experience, Murray wrote letters to his family, saying that he was "happy and thoroughly well." Unable to believe that he could be happy in such circumstances, his family thought he must have gone mad, but he reassured them: "I have not lost my reason, but all worries, anxieties, and frustrations." He described "an undivided mind, inner stillness, self-realization, and a fullness that I never believed possible."[7]

Murray's new positivity encouraged him to rewrite his mountaineering book, even though there was a high risk that it would be discovered and lost again. As conditions worsened at the camp during the final period of the war, he and the other inmates were close to starvation, but he managed to finish the book. Exhilarated by his creativity and his spiritual studies, he wrote, "During this last year, I had not once thought of myself as imprisoned." He later reflected that "those prison years were the most productive of my life."[8]

Against all odds, both Murray and his book survived the war. He returned to the Scottish mountains to recover from his ordeal and seriously contemplated joining a monastery. However, his book *Mountaineering in Scotland* was soon accepted by a publisher, and he realized that he had a new career as an author. Putting aside the idea of becoming of a monk, he decided that the mountains would be his monastery, his source of spiritual sustenance. He became a well-known climber, in the Himalayas as well as in Scotland, and wrote many books on mountaineering and travel, as well as a number of novels.

Murray's story recalls a powerful awakening experience described by the Hungarian-British author Arthur Koestler. As a young man in the 1930s, Koestler was living in Paris as a communist activist and journalist. During the Spanish Civil War, he traveled to Spain as a war correspondent and was arrested by Spanish nationalists. As a known communist activist, he was charged with espionage and sentenced to death. While in solitary confinement, waiting for his sentence to be carried out, he passed the time scratching mathematical formulae on the wall with a metal spring he had taken out of his mattress. It struck him that the formulae represented objective, eternal truths, glimpses into an infinite realm that lay beyond human affairs. This insight filled him with awe, which led to an intense awakening experience:

> I was floating on my back in a river of peace, under bridges of silence. It came from nowhere and flowed nowhere. Then there was no river and no I. The I had ceased to exist....
>
> [For] the first time the veil has fallen and one is in touch with "real reality," the hidden order of things, the X-ray texture of the world, normally obscured by layers of irrelevancy.
>
> The "I" ceases to exist because it has ... been dissolved in the universal pool. It is the process of dissolution and limitless expansion which is sensed as the "oceanic feeling," as the draining of all tension, the absolute catharsis, the peace that passeth all understanding.[9]

Koestler wasn't sure whether this initial experience lasted for minutes or hours, but for days afterward a feeling of peace remained. Occasionally the full intensity of the original experience returned too, initially at least once or twice a week.

After several months in prison — following intense lobbying by his British wife — Koestler was freed in a prisoner exchange. Following his release, he continued to have occasional awakening experiences and felt that he had undergone a permanent change. As he put in his memoir *The Invisible Writing*, "the groundwork for a change or personality was completed."[10]

Political Prisoners

What constitutes a crime varies from society to society. In totalitarian societies, as the Soviet dissident Aleksandr Solzhenitsyn wrote, "a mere thought [is] punishable." It is a crime to have opinions that differ from government propaganda, and any expression of such opinions is likely to bring imprisonment. In some societies — usually those with totalitarian governments — it is a crime simply to belong to a particular ethnic group or religion. In other societies, even though they may not be overtly oppressive or authoritarian, people who behave in unusual ways or perceive the world in a way that is not considered normal may be labeled mad and incarcerated in institutions. As the French philosopher Michel Foucault showed, throughout history ruling elites have used prisons and insane asylums to exert their authority and to punish and incarcerate anyone who potentially threatens their power.

Every authoritarian society, from Nazi Germany to Soviet Russia and modern-day North Korea, has used prison camps in this way. In Eastern Europe after the Second World War, communist countries sent millions of their citizens to prisons, or to specially built labor camps, simply because those citizens weren't prepared to passively accept a life of oppression and tyranny.

Mihajlo Mihajlov was a Yugoslavian citizen who was punished for his thoughts. After the Second World War, Yugoslavia became a communist country, under the rule of President Tito. Born in 1934, Mihajlov became a professor of Russian literature at Belgrade University. As a strong-minded free thinker, he dared to criticize the government. His dissent stemmed from his spirituality. Although he never went to church and wasn't attached to any conventional Christian group, he was strongly influenced by the teachings of Jesus, which he saw as representing a genuine socialism, including freedom of speech and democracy. Mihajlov was painfully aware of how far short Tito's regime fell of these ideals and publicly voiced his misgivings. He was accused of spreading "enemy propaganda" and spent seven years in prison.

After his release, Mihajlov was inspired to write an important essay titled "Freedom in the Gulag: Spiritual Lessons of the Concentration Camp." Discussing the inmates of Soviet gulags — but surely also referring to his own experiences — Mihajlov described how the loss of freedom could lead to intense awakening experiences:

> Although under these conditions they had to endure the worst form of psychic and physical suffering, they experienced at the same time moments of utter happiness, such as those outside the camp walls could never imagine. Never before had they felt love, hate, and despair so strongly ... never felt so at one with the universe, as during their time in prison.[11]

According to Mihajlov, as the inmates' physical health declined, their inner life became more intense. If they were prepared to let go of attachment to the body, a powerful soul-force would arise inside them, which not only brought them spiritual well-being but also helped to keep them alive in the face of starvation, subzero temperatures, and disease. It enabled them to become stronger than "all outward forces of oppression and destruction."[12] Mihajlov described this soul-force in supernatural terms:

> When a man has got rid of all that ties him, a mysterious thing happens: In the depths of his soul there rises up a mighty force which not only endows his totally exhausted body with incredible powers of resistance, but, in strange ways which we do not yet fully understand, also begins to affect the visible world.[13]

The powers described by Mihajlov are very similar to the Hindu concept of the *siddhis*, the supernatural powers that, according to yogic philosophy, arise at higher levels of spiritual development. Among the various types of *siddhis* is one involving control of the body's functions. There have been numerous reports of yogis who were able to regulate their body temperature, keeping themselves warm in freezing conditions, and others who could bring themselves back from the point of death or keep themselves alive and healthy without food or water.

While living through the horrors of Auschwitz, the psychiatrist Viktor Frankl observed that his fellow concentration camp inmates were more likely to survive if they felt they had a goal or purpose. Frankl's own purpose was to rewrite the book manuscript that was confiscated when he was taken into the camp, scribbling key words in shorthand on scraps of paper and memorizing passages. (This is very similar to Bill Murray's story above. Frankl's book was also published shortly after the end of the war.) Frankl attributed his own survival largely to his strong sense of purpose. However, time and again, he saw others give up hope or lose connection to their ideals or goals, as a result of which they became vulnerable to disease and death. As Frankl wrote, "Woe to him who saw no more sense to life. He was soon lost."[14]

Perhaps the soul-force — or *siddhi* — described by Mihajlov is another factor explaining the survival of some of the inmates of gulags and concentration camps. A person who underwent spiritual transformation in the midst of their deprivation and suffering would surely have a greater chance of survival — partly because of an attitude of acceptance and trust but also perhaps because of the protective physical effects of soul-force. Solzhenitsyn, one of the gulag survivors referred to by Mihajlov, described how a "strange inner warmth" saved him from freezing to death during the Siberian winter. Another Russian dissident author who was sent to the gulags, Dimitrii Mikhailovich Panin, described how a mysterious force brought him back to life when he was thought to be dead. This experience led Panin to write, "Save your soul, and you'll save your body too."[15]

These abilities certainly sound very similar to *siddhis*. And perhaps, since the *siddhis* arise at higher levels of spiritual development, they also offer evidence that these inmates underwent spiritual transformation.

Irina Ratushinskaya

In Soviet Russia to be a poet was a dangerous occupation. Poetry was associated with dissent and rebellion, and many of the greatest Russian poets of the twentieth century were sent to the gulags. In 1983 this was the fate of a young poet named Irina Ratushinskaya, arrested on charges of "anti-Soviet agitation and propaganda" after circulating collections of her poems. Ratushinskaya was sentenced to seven years' hard labor, followed by five years of internal exile.

Soon after arriving at the gulag, Ratushinskaya began a campaign of what she called "holy disobedience," in protest against the inhumane conditions. As a result, she was singled out for especially harsh treatment and placed in a "small zone" reserved for "particularly dangerous female political criminals." Although it was just a short time before the era of glasnost and the end of the Soviet Union, she was treated with appalling brutality. For four years she endured beatings, torture, a near-starvation diet, freezing winter temperatures, and long periods of solitary confinement.

In spite of these terrible conditions, Ratushinskaya continued writing poetry in secret. She wrote 250 poems during her confinement, scratching them out on bars of soap so that she could wash them away if a guard came her way. She would memorize the lines and then write them out in tiny letters on cigarette papers, which were smuggled out of the gulag by her husband on his visits. Her poetry depicts what she described as "the enormous capacity of the human spirit to be happy in spite of any circumstances." In her poem "Believe Me," she wrote, "In solitary cells, on winter nights / A sudden sense of joy and warmth / And a resounding note of love."[16]

As her physical condition deteriorated, Ratushinskaya felt the same intense spiritual power described by Mihajlov. She wrote, "When you don't own even your own body, you come to understand that you *do* own your own soul." She came close to death several times due to illness and hunger and developed a certainty of some form of life after death: "Being close to death you can feel there's something beyond."[17] This wasn't just a belief based on wishful thinking but an awareness of an essence of her being that was formless and deathless.

As well as showing her incredible resilience and paradoxical contentment, Ratushinskaya's poems display an amazing intensity of perception. Even in such a bleak and brutal environment, she was able to find beauty. In her poem "I Will Live and Survive," she described the patterns on a frost-covered window with the same kind of awe and ecstasy that other poets have described mountain landscapes or flowers. This poem also describes the transformational effects of perceiving such intense beauty:

> A frost-covered window! No spy-holes, nor walls,
> Nor cell-bars, nor the long endured pain —
> Only a blue radiance on a tiny pane of glass,
> A cast pattern — none more beautiful could be dreamt!
> The more clearly you looked the more powerfully blossomed
> Those brigand forests, campfires and birds! ...
>
> Such a gift can only be received once,
> And perhaps is only needed once.[18]

Perhaps most remarkably, although she protested against conditions at the camp, Ratushinskaya felt no hatred toward her interrogators. Sensing that hatred and bitterness would damage her psychologically, she decided not to allow them to fester. Instead she empathized with her interrogators, imagining them as fathers whose children might one day play with hers. She felt sorry for them, reasoning that she might be released, whereas they might have to stay in the camp for the rest of their lives. As she said in an interview after her release from the camp, "You must not hate. I only understood this in labor camp. To decide not to hate is not just to have mercy on your interrogators but also on yourself."[19]

While she was imprisoned, some of Ratushinskaya's poems were published, leading to international outcry at her treatment. This led to her release by Mikhail Gorbachev in 1986. She lived in England and the United States but eventually returned to Russia, where she lived until her death in 2017.

The Case of Sri Aurobindo

Perhaps the most significant example of a political prisoner who underwent spiritual awakening is Sri Aurobindo. His story is so significant because, after his awakening, he became one of the greatest spiritual teachers and authors of the twentieth century.

Sri Aurobindo is one of my favorite spiritual authors because he is a rare example of a powerful intellect combined with a high intensity of wakefulness. He used his sharp intellect to observe and analyze his own higher states of consciousness and to examine their implications for human development. This led to his magnum opus, *The Life Divine*, which established a link between higher states of consciousness (such as those we examine throughout this book) and the future stages of evolution.

Sri Aurobindo's main insight was that what present-day human beings experience as higher states of consciousness are glimpses of the future of evolution and will one day be normal to the whole human race. Aurobindo believed that a new phase of human evolution is unfolding, with the emergence of a new type of human being he called the "gnostic being" who possesses "new forces of thought and sight and a power of direct spiritual realization."[20] (The extraordinary awakenings of this book can be seen as examples of the unfolding of this new type of consciousness, while the shifters themselves could be seen as examples of "gnostic beings." This is an area I'll examine in more detail in the last chapter of this book.)

Sri Aurobindo wrote many other great works too, developing a spiritual practice that he called "integral yoga," through which human life could be raised to the level of "divine life."

However, before he became a spiritual teacher and author, Sri Aurobindo — or Aurobindo Ghose, as he was known then — was a political activist and a political prisoner. As a young man, he was inspired by the cause of Indian nationalism and became a leading figure in the protests against British colonial rule. At one point the British authorities called him "the most dangerous man in India." At the age of thirty-six he was arrested by the British authorities for treason after a bomb attack by an organization he was linked to. There was no evidence against Aurobindo personally, but he was sent to prison, where he remained for around a year.

Up until that point, Aurobindo's main goal had been to change his country rather than himself. The external goals of politics had monopolized his attention. However, not long before his arrest, he had taken up meditation and yoga as an aid to his political work, hoping that they would strengthen his resilience and increase his energy. He went to see a yogi for instruction and had an awakening experience while sitting and meditating with him. He briefly experienced a state of pure, formless consciousness in which there was "only just absolutely That, featureless, relationless, sheer, indescribable, unthinkable, absolute, yet supremely real and solely real." During this experience he felt an "inexpressible peace, a stupendous silence, an infinity of release and freedom."[21]

This was a prelude to the profound transformation that Aurobindo experienced during his year in prison. He published an account of his imprisonment as *Tales of Prison Life*, which is especially interesting because, in reflecting on his spiritual awakening, he explicitly described prison life in monastic terms. He was fully aware that for him the solitude, quietness, and detachment of prison were equivalent to a long period of monastic retreat, a period that permanently transformed his being: "Though I have described it as 'imprisonment' for a year, it was, in effect, like a year's seclusion as in an *Ashram* or hermitage.... This *yogashram* happened to be the British prison.... The British Government's wrath had but one significant outcome: I found God."[22]

Conditions in the prison were appalling. Aurobindo spent long periods in solitary confinement in a tiny cell (about five foot by nine foot) with two tar-coated baskets as his toilet. The baskets were cleaned out only in the mornings and evenings, resulting in a continual smell of urine and feces. There was no ventilation, and the heat was overwhelming. At times there was only a small amount of lukewarm water to drink. Food was minimal too — usually just rice and lentils. There was no bed, just a couple of blankets on top of the stone floor. Not surprisingly, Aurobindo found it difficult to sleep, and even when he did, he was often woken up by the shouting of sentries.

Aurobindo continued to practice meditation and yoga, as he had learned to do shortly before his arrest. He meditated for long periods, even though he found that his mind was restless and difficult to control. When he was first put into solitary confinement, he felt anxious, since he wasn't used to solitude and inactivity. He was afraid of losing control of his thoughts and going mad. After a few days of solitude, he feared that this was actually happening. He was "barraged by an endless stream of thoughts. Suddenly the thoughts became incoherent as if the mind had lost its control over them.... I was so terrified of losing my mental balance."[23] This was when a shift occurred. He was so desperate that he prayed for help from God. In *Tales of Prison Life*, he described what suddenly happened next:

> A great peace descended upon my mind and heart. A cooling sensation spread over my entire body. The restless mind became relaxed and joyful. I experienced a state of indescribable bliss. I felt as if I was lying on the lap of the World-Mother just as a child

does, with a sense of complete security and utter ease. From that very moment, my suffering in prison evaporated....Subsequent hardships in prison like restlessness or mental unease...or physical suffering or illness or despair in the process of yoga sadhana, were met with an imperturbable poise. The intelligence was able to derive strength and joy from the sorrow itself and annul the suffering of the mind. Therefore hardships seemed as if drops of water on a lily.[24]

Aurobindo spent the rest of his imprisonment in a state of bliss. After a while, he was given permission to go for a walk every day, in a narrow space between the prison and a cowshed. As he walked, he would recite mantras from the Upanishads, and everything that he saw appeared as an expression of what the Upanishads call *brahman*, or universal spirit:

I would attain a state where the perception of reality was no longer defined by the prison and its commonplace objects. The high enclosure, the iron bars, the blank surface of the wall, the tree with its green leaves shining in the sunlight – all seemed to come alive as if animated by a universal consciousness. A vibration of pure love seemed to radiate from them towards me. All of creation seemed to be just Nature's elaborate play, whilst a vast, pure, detached spirit, rapt in a serene delight, looked out from within....These experiences overwhelmed my body and mind. A pure and wide peace reigned everywhere; it was an indescribable state. The hard crust of my exterior personality was removed, thus enabling a free outflow of love for all creatures from within. Other Sattwic elements such as charity, kindness and Ahimsa began to now dominate the Rajasic bent of my nature. As the Sattwic aspects gained more prominence in the personality, the sense of delight intensified and the peace too deepened.[25]

After a year of incarceration, Aurobindo was released without charge. His political colleagues expected him to continue to fight for their cause, but now he was a different person. Political issues no longer seemed important. It no longer seemed enough to help liberate his country. Now he wanted to serve the whole human race, to help liberate all human beings from psychological suffering. Most of all, he wanted to help manifest the next stage in the evolution of human consciousness. And he devoted the rest of his life to this goal.

The Ascetic Way

Throughout this chapter, we've looked at cases of people who were stripped of everything, deprived of all essential human needs — food and shelter, safety and security, self-esteem and respect. We have seen cases of people who were mentally and physically tortured to the point where they were psychologically broken and physically close to death. And at the point of complete desolation, pared down to their barest essence, the prisoners made an amazing discovery. At the essence of their being, they found a new, awakened self waiting to emerge, like a bird from the shattered pieces of its shell.

We've already drawn parallels between the life of prisoners and that of monks, but there is another approach to spiritual development that resembles the extreme deprivation of prisoners of war and political prisoners. This is the tradition of asceticism, in which spiritual seekers voluntarily inflict pain and discomfort on themselves. In the Indian yogic tradition, this is known as *tapas*. *Tapas* (which literally means "heat" in Sanskrit) entails leading a life of purposeful hardship, including fasting, prolonged standing, exposure to extreme temperatures, and celibacy.

Asceticism was practiced by many early Christians, who forced themselves to live in extremely harsh conditions. They would fast for long periods, expose themselves to the cold in winter, and wear hair shirts. For example, Saint Simeon Stylites, who lived in Syria in the fifth century, ate only once a week, wore a rope of palm leaves twisted around his body, and went completely without food or drink during Lent. The fourteenth-century German mystic Henry de Suso spent years wearing a hair shirt and an iron chain, as well as a belt containing 150 inward-facing sharp brass nails. St. Francis of Assisi was the son of a wealthy merchant but chose to give up everything for a life of homelessness, poverty, hard work, and service. He lived as a homeless beggar and spent years doing harsh manual labor.

No doubt many ascetics were motivated by a perverse and neurotic self-hatred, rooted in an unhealthy sense of division between the spirit and the body and a desire to control and punish the body because of its "unclean" desires. But some ascetics must have had a genuine impulse for spiritual growth. In its healthiest sense, asceticism is a path of purgation or purification. Some ascetics were attempting to pare themselves down to their essence so that they could experience the naked, empty state described above by Sri Aurobindo and Mihajlo Mihajlov. In a sense, they were trying to consciously create the conditions of a gulag or wartime prison camp, in the hope that they could uncover the soul-force described by Mihajlov and undergo spiritual awakening.[26]

The process is essentially the same in both imprisonment and asceticism. When intense deprivation and suffering (whether or not it is consciously inflicted) strip us of our desires, our attachments, and our identity, an extraordinary awakening can occur.

3

FREEDOM IN PRISON, PART TWO

Transformation through Incarceration

Alister Hardy was a marine biologist at Oxford University with a lifelong interest in spirituality and a belief that spiritual experiences should be studied scientifically. Toward the end of his academic career, in 1969, he set up the Religious Experience Research Unit at Oxford University. (It is now based at the University of Wales in Lampeter.) Hardy began to collect and analyze reports of religious and spiritual experiences via newspaper and magazine adverts. The standard question he asked was "Have you ever been aware of or influenced by a presence or power, whether you called it God or not, that is different from your everyday self?"

In the early 1980s, a researcher named Ann Wetherall was working with Hardy, helping him to categorize the large number of reports they were sent. (At present, the database contains more than sixty-five hundred reports.) Noticing that a significant number of reports were from prisoners, Wetherall decided to follow up with a research project focusing specifically on prisoners' spiritual experiences. After placing ads in prison newspapers, she received a large number of responses, with many correspondents writing that it was the first time they had ever told anyone about their spiritual experiences. They had never talked about them for fear of being thought crazy and being sent to see a psychiatrist.

One response was from an inmate of a Borstal (a young offenders' prison in the UK) who had a powerful experience while on a hunger strike. The man was from an Irish Catholic background and so used Christian concepts to interpret his experience:

> I suddenly felt the most holy benediction flood my heart with a physical warmth so comforting, so absolutely unworldly that I felt my sins (which were many and grievous) were wiped away....As the feeling gradually matured in me, all my lifelong grief and sadness, all the loneliness and self-recrimination, all the hate was washed away and healed. In their place was the Holy Ghost. It did not go away. It remained there where the physical heart is like an infinitely tender and live warmth-cum-light. It expressed itself as Life and Intelligence and Love — all in One. Words are inadequate to describe the experience. It can only be expressed by living one's life consistently in a way that can express one's gratitude and admiration, love and loyalty to it.[1]

The description of "holy benediction" is reminiscent of the soul-force described by Mihajlo Mihajlov, as mentioned in the last chapter. Since the experience occurred on the fifty-eighth day of his hunger strike, the man must have been in a state of physical debilitation similar to that of the gulag inmates. As the report suggests, the experience wasn't just temporary but initiated a permanent shift. The man abandoned his hunger strike and adopted a more cooperative attitude, feeling a new sense of acceptance of his predicament. Unfortunately, there isn't much detail about his life after his release, although we're told that he gave up drinking and smoking and embarked on a different way of life.

After receiving such a large number of reports, Wetherall decided to start an initiative to support prisoners, partly to help reassure them they weren't mad but also to nurture their spiritual development. This was the Prison-Ashram Project, founded in 1988 to give prisoners access to meditation, yoga, and spiritual work-shops and books. Now called the Prison Phoenix Trust, the orga-nization is still flourishing. It runs yoga and meditation classes in eighty-two secure institutions around the UK, supporting around 8 percent of the UK's total prison population. At the core of the trust's philosophy is the idea that prison offers an *opportunity* for spiritual growth — that is, an environment where spiritual growth is more likely to occur than in normal, everyday environments.

The Prison Phoenix Trust receives a steady flow of letters and emails from prisoners who describe the positive effects of their yoga and meditation sessions. Many of the letters are published in the trust's quarterly newsletter. Some prisoners report that they are sleeping better, feeling calmer and happier, that they have given up smoking or cut down on (or even given up) medication. Others de-scribe how meditation and yoga have changed their behavior and attitude, making them less self-centered, more tolerant and patient, less emotionally reactive.

One person serving time for theft described feeling surprised by his reaction when he saw a watch fall out of someone's pocket in front of him. Rather than pocketing the watch himself, he heard himself say to the man, "Hey — you've dropped your watch." He felt that this signified a major change, which he was sure was due to meditation. Another prisoner described a similar sense of surprise when he spent three days trying to release a moth from his cell win-dow, when previously he would have killed it without thinking.

Other prisoners describe deep-rooted inner changes that sug-gest some degree of spiritual awakening. They describe an awareness of a more essential self, beyond their environmental conditioning and their habitual behavior. One prisoner spoke of "finding the real me, letting go and shedding all the garbage I'd collected over the years." Another person described "feeling at last a connection with my inner self. Nothing matters, I'm carefree, empty of worries, and consumed by positive energy, content with who I am." Another correspondent commented, "There is a deeper me who is not that ego and is kind, compassionate, and cares about people."

There are also some reports of powerful awakening experiences in some of the trust's newsletters. One prisoner described sitting outside meditating when he heard the flapping of wings and opened his eyes. He saw a crow and felt that he was inside the bird, and that in fact he *was* the crow. Another person described how, after a few weeks of practicing meditation, he saw a flower that seemed so powerfully vivid it was as if it were calling for his attention. He looked at a tree, which seemed to be calling to him in the same way. Everything he looked at seemed incredibly real and beautiful.

With some prisoners, these experiences were ongoing. One prisoner described regular experiences of oneness during meditation in which "there's just a still pool of consciousness without a ripple on its surface." Another person spoke of being able to "tune in to emptiness": "Sometimes I feel an expansion that goes out in all directions, way beyond the walls.... It feels like everything, the trees outside, the walls, in fact the whole jail and my body is being held by emptiness."[2]

The Power of Quietness, Inactivity, and Solitude

All these accounts are a great advertisement for the power of meditation and yoga. But they are also testament to the high spiritual potential of imprisonment. As we have already seen — and as Ann Wetherall realized — some aspects of incarceration predispose people to spiritual development and awakening experiences. I mentioned the two main reasons for the high spiritual potential of imprisonment at the beginning of the last chapter: the dissolution of psychological attachments and a large amount of inactivity and solitude. In particular, I think that the accounts of the prisoners above are a testament to the spiritual potential of inactivity and solitude, which enabled the prisoners to connect to their essential, unconditioned selves for the first time.

In ordinary life we human beings spend very little time with ourselves. We are almost always immersed in activities and entertainments. When we aren't busy performing tasks, we switch our attention to smartphones or computer games or text messages or TV screens. As I put it in my book *Back to Sanity*, we live in a state of "elsewhereness" in which we rarely give our attention to the present or to our own inner being. We spend so much time *doing* that we leave almost no time for *being*.

As a result, many of us are estranged from our true selves. We end up living inauthentically, playing roles and following conventions for the sake of others, disconnected from our deepest impulses. We also end up living superficially, immersed in the cramped space of the ego rather than exploring the richness and depths of our being. Our alienation from our real selves also creates a sense of discord — a constant feeling of unease, as if something essential is missing, although we can't pinpoint what it is.

To be cut off from ordinary society and all its distractions, and to be obliged to turn our attention to our own being, can therefore prove to be a powerful experience. For most people, it is simply a painful experience, exposing them to psychological discord on the surface of their minds. But for others — such as the prisoners quoted above — it may lead to a profound encounter with their real selves, beneath the surface discord.

In this way, quietness and inactivity may have a powerful therapeutic effect. They can dissolve away our stress and replace it with a sense of inner harmony. By enabling us to go beneath the mind's surface discord, they put us in touch with a rich spiritual energy that has a natural quality of well-being.

This is one of the reasons we go on spiritual retreats, and why many people love solitary pursuits such as climbing (as in the case of Bill Murray in the last chapter) and sailing. We might feel a similar sense of inner harmony on vacations too, when we allow ourselves to stop rushing and worrying and spend time relaxing and doing nothing. For a short space of time, we switch into a mode of being rather than doing.

I first wrote about the healing power of quietness and solitude in *Back to Sanity*. There I told the story of an Australian man named Paul Narada Alister. Alister spent seven years in prison after being falsely convicted of a terrorist attack, before being pardoned. At first he found the lack of stimulation difficult to cope with, but once he had adjusted to his predicament, he began to relish his solitude and inactivity. He spent most of his time meditating and contemplating and began to feel enriched with a new feeling of aliveness. He was filled with "a deep sense of freedom and positivity," which made his wrongful imprisonment not only bearable but beneficial:

> The inner silence that prison afforded me gave me an experience I carry to this day. I no longer avoid solitude or isolation. If anything I look forward to [them] as a time to experience that inner silence which can give me so much bliss. Be it in meditation or just enjoying my own company, I find silence is golden when experienced as a way to get in touch with my spiritual self.[3]

Nelson Mandela — probably the most well-known political prisoner of all time — also experienced the therapeutic power of solitude and quietness in prison. I don't feel confident in saying that Mandela had a full-fledged spiritual awakening during his twenty-seven years in captivity, since he doesn't discuss such an experience in his autobiography (although of course it's possible that he simply chose not to disclose it). However, there seems no doubt that Mandela did undergo significant psychological development, leading to a deep-rooted change in his personality. He became more reflective, calmer, and more compassionate. In his letters from prison, he wrote a good deal about the benefits he gained from his solitude and inactivity. As he wrote, "The cell is an ideal place to learn to know yourself, to search realistically and regularly the process of your own mind and feelings."[4]

"It Was Like the Flick of a Switch" – Adrian's Story

Another testament to the spiritual potential of quietness and self-exploration was shared with me by a British man named Adrian Troy.

Born in 1963, Adrian lived an adventurous life as a marine, a pearl diver, a sailor, and a captain, mostly in Australia and Asia. In 2010 he took a temporary job for a security company operating in the Red Sea, off the coast of Africa, protecting ships against piracy. Four days into the job, he and three other crew members were arrested by the Eritrean Navy. The authorities had discovered an illegal stash of weapons belonging to the security company. Adrian's ship was shot at by the navy, and as captain, he stood before pointed and loaded rifles, expecting to be shot.

Adrian and his shipmates were incarcerated for six months, locked up in the same room twenty-three hours a day, in complete isolation from the outside world. The room was so small that there was no space for them to walk or exercise. They were accused of invasion and espionage, due to the illegal activities of the security company, and had no idea how long they would be kept in prison. They had no access to legal assistance and didn't go through any legal process of prosecution. As Adrian told me, "It was a desperate situation with much mental angst. Unfortunately, two of my cell mates were in huge mental pain and came close to meltdown. Unlike me, they knew about the company's illegal activities, but they couldn't accept their own responsibility."

Their captors allowed them to keep a few personal items, and Adrian had a statuette of the Buddha that he had picked up on his travels in Asia. During the endless hours of incarceration, the statuette became his focus. He told me, "It gave me a lot of inspiration. I never asked or pleaded for anything but talked to the Buddha as a calming and accepting influence."

Although he had never meditated or followed any kind of spiritual practice before, Adrian developed a spontaneous meditation practice, silently focusing his attention on the statuette for long periods. He also began to reflect on his life and to let go of the past and any sense of failure or disappointment. Whereas his cell mates were in a state of turmoil, Adrian accepted his predicament and his own responsibility for it: "My meditation theme was acceptance and release of everything. My silent words to myself were 'I'm here because someone has to be here.'"

Over the next few weeks, as his meditation continued, Adrian began to feel more at peace, until he experienced a sudden shift:

It was like the flick of a switch. It happened in an instant, on March 21, 2011. Without anticipation, expectancy, or planning, my mind and body entered a state of relaxed bliss that I can describe as euphoric stillness. My mind was empty of all chatter. It was as if I was floating out of my body. It was otherworldly, like walking into a different dimension. It was a complete feeling of release and acceptance, of everything and anything that was going to happen. It was a release of blame, of anxiety, of anger and ego.

I didn't understand what was happening. I don't have a religious or spiritual background. I didn't have any knowledge of meditation, yoga, or mind disciplines. But for three days I was in a state of what can best be described as grace, with a sense of intense euphoria. After that, the feeling eased, but it remained inside me.

Seven weeks later, Adrian and his crew were released and returned to England. With his expanded and intensified awareness, he felt like he was looking at the world with new eyes:

I had a very surreal feeling, as if I was floating. Things were moving in slow motion, and I felt I was five seconds ahead of time.

This reality didn't seem real. Sometimes I felt confused and a bit scared, then at other times there was a huge sense of well-being. I was in a hotel in London, and the city seemed magical. I could literally feel the history of the buildings. On the tube I looked at people and could see and feel their energy. I could almost see what they were thinking from their eyes and expressions. Everything seemed to emit its own energy and frequency – buildings, bricks, a pint of beer, a seashell, a park bench, and so on.

Walking in nature was amazing. I was hypnotized by flowers, trees, leaves. They looked beautiful and surreal and filled me with warm love. I would gaze at rolling green hills, woods, natural rocky landscapes and feel a sense of near ecstasy.

Without a background in spirituality, Adrian wasn't sure what had happened to him. He went through periods of doubting his sanity. He even wondered if he had caught rabies while in Africa. He read about PTSD and schizophrenia and other psychiatric conditions, searching for a diagnosis, but found that his symptoms didn't match. Other people thought he had gone mad too and began to distance themselves from him. As he told me, "Many people fell out of my life. I was no longer the old me. Some people thought I'd lost my marbles, when in fact I'd found them! Some of my closest old friends got it, but others said I should see a psychiatrist."

Despite his difficulties, Adrian knew deep down that he was undergoing a powerful positive experience. And eventually, he began to make sense of his transformation. Six months after his release from prison, he accidentally discovered a spiritual book called *A Step into the Light* by Peter L. Martinez. The book provided a context for his transformation and reassured him that he wasn't mad.

Following this, Adrian gradually began to adjust to his new intense awareness, which no longer seemed so overwhelming and destabilizing. Speaking nine years after his shift, he told me:

It's settled down now and has integrated and changed my life. I have a feeling of absolute love and protection! I became a more gentle person with much more empathy. I pick up and detect people's emotions quite strongly. In the presence of darker energy from people I have to walk away. I feel a new connection to animals. Sometimes I feel like I've become a magnet for dogs and cats. They just know something's different.

I've become sensitive to the cycle of the moon and more aware of the planets too. I love to see Venus shining as the evening or morning star. My eating habits have changed too. I became a vegetarian. I lost weight – in a healthy way – and started looking very healthy, with clear eyes, with a vibrancy that other people noticed.

During this process I began to have an interest in all religions. I realized that enlightened human beings – Jesus, Zoroaster, Muhammad, Buddha, Lao Tzu, Rumi – all had the same message. Many tributaries but the same beautiful source. I read Eckhart Tolle's *The Power of Now* a few years after my transformation, and the story of his awakening left me saying, "Yes, yes, yes!" Eckhart's writings confirmed what I already felt.

When I got back to England, some people didn't understand why I wasn't bitter about what happened, why I didn't feel any anger or hatred. But it was a massive gift. It gave me much more than I could ever have imagined.

"I Just Kept Letting Go" – Ananta's Story

The story we're going to hear now is an even more powerful example of the awakening effects of the isolation and deprivation of the prison environment and of how being stripped of identity can lead to the birth of a new spiritual self.

Ananta Kranti's story is different from Adrian's — and most of the others in this book — in the sense that she had some knowledge and experience of spirituality before her transformation. She had already become a dedicated spiritual seeker before she went to prison. Her transformational experience in prison changed her from a seeker to a finder.

Like many people who undergo spiritual awakening, Ananta had a difficult early life, with dysfunction and discord in her family. At the age of nineteen she went on vacation to Spain and decided not to return. She didn't have any money or anywhere to stay, but she had trust and a free spirit, and was streetwise. She lived a hand-to-mouth existence, working for clubs or giving massages (without any sexual aspects) and sometimes sleeping outdoors. After a few months, she fell in love with a rich Saudi Arabian man who became her partner of ten years. Unfortunately, he introduced her to hard drugs. She had previously taken LSD and smoked marijuana, but now she began to take cocaine and later heroin:

> After a few years with the Arab guy, I was addicted to and taking heroin with him and sunk into such a deep hole. There was loads of money, but I was so depressed. I was seeing through the illusion of the material world. My partner was a billionaire and he was deeply unhappy. That ended my search for material happiness. It ignited my call for true freedom. As my material search ended, my spiritual search became conscious.

Ananta had saved up some money and decided to go to Thailand to heal and get off heroin. There she felt the same sense of release as when she had left England a few years earlier, and she decided not to return to Spain. From Thailand she traveled to Japan, after hearing that there was a demand for young European girls — particularly girls with blond hair and blue eyes like her — to work as hostesses in businessmen's clubs. The job was so well paid that she only needed to work for three months and was free the rest of the year. She stayed in Japan for several years, living a hedonistic life but with a growing awareness that this way of life couldn't bring happiness:

> It really became apparent that no matter how free I was, there was something inside that needed an answer. All the parties, all the love affairs, and all the Ecstasy we were taking at that time

just pointed to depression. There was something missing, something that needed an answer. It started me on a quest to find that something deeper. Someone gave me a book by Osho. As soon as I read that book, it was like an explosion. There was an immediate recognition that what he was speaking about was the answer to this call.

Ananta felt called to move away from hedonism and her drug connections and to follow a spiritual way of life. She left Japan for Osho's community in India, determined to empty herself of all her conditioning and embrace inner silence. After months of spiritual practice, she took *Sannyas* (spiritual vows) to surrender all the past and take on a new spiritual life. (This is where she was given the name Ananta.)

At this point, Ananta was prepared to give up everything and immerse herself completely in her new spiritual life. However, she was running short of money and so decided to go back to Japan to do one final stint as a hostess. Shortly after her arrival, a friend in London contacted her to say that she had a large amount of high-quality LSD. Coincidentally, Ananta had heard about a man who was looking for some LSD and mentioned this to her friend. Without letting her know in advance, her friend flew over to Japan and arrived on her doorstep with the LSD. However, the potential deal didn't happen. Ananta's friend stayed at her flat temporarily then had to leave Tokyo for a while. She asked if she could leave the LSD with Ananta for the time being, and she agreed.

Five days later, police raided Ananta's flat and found the LSD. She was taken into custody and spent the next three years incarcerated, in conditions much more severe than those of any European prison. Prisoners weren't allowed to speak and worked long hours in terrible conditions in a factory, as if they were slaves. The guards treated them with contempt and cruelty. Ananta was also the only Westerner in her prison block, which made her more of a target and added to her sense of isolation.

However, the hardship and trauma of her imprisonment led to a dramatic awakening:

In the silence of the prison, there was a lot of mental aggression and violence. It was hard-core. A lot of the other prisoners were in there for murder. Some of them had been in there for fifteen years or more, and I could feel their anger and hatred.

The work at the factory was incredibly hard. Whatever we did one day, we had to do better the next. We were counted eight times a day like soldiers. I sometimes had the chance to whisper, but we weren't allowed to speak. We weren't allowed any exercise, although eventually they let us do thirty minutes a day in our cells.

After months of this, I was broken on every level. I was at the exhaustion point, in terrible mental and physical pain. All I had in my cell was some Osho books that a friend had given me during my trial. I would read a couple of pages after coming back from the factory, and the wisdom would go deep inside me, directly and immediately.

One day I came back to the cell from the factory and was just about to start reading but couldn't. I was in too much pain. I lay back and dropped into the pain. I knew how to do that because of the bodywork I'd done. I knew how to breathe into the pain and go deeper and deeper. But the pain in my body was so severe that it was painful to relax. I lay back and kept dropping and dropping into the pain. It was excruciating, but I had to surrender to it. There was nothing else left to do.

Then I dropped into a space where the physical body was no more. Whatever I dropped into just kept opening and opening, into more and more light, beauty, gratitude, freedom....I just kept letting go and dropping and dropping. There was only this – this beautiful love and bliss.

I started to go there every night. I would lie down and drop into this freedom. Before then my mind had been going crazy, thinking continuously, looking at the calendar and trying to work out when I might be released, since we were never given a date. I would look at the calendar all night long in my cell instead of sleeping. But now there was a shift into acceptance. Gratitude lifted me into another space, and there was no problem. I started to see the joke of everything. There was an inner smile. I had a feeling of "they've taken everything, but they can't take this." They couldn't take the inner silence and bliss away from me.

It was the death of who I was, with more and more surrender. All the roles fell away. And it grew more and more. I was in a constant state of bliss, even though the same conditions and difficulties continued in prison. When I ate, I would go higher and higher until I felt I became the food. I felt connected with its growth and the whole process of preparing it. I rose above the greed into a place of gratitude and bliss, and I hardly needed to eat anything at all.

When we were marched into the factory in the mornings, I would see the sun over the horizon and hear the sounds of the birds, and it was so beautiful. I saw the value in the tiniest things. All I could do was be with the miracle of the moment. I was just in the moment and had made peace with where I was. When you realize that you have a freedom that can't be taken away, all things become precious and beautiful.

I started to see the guards who were so brutal as if they were the prisoners. I felt sorry for them, because I was going to get out at some point, and they would still be here. I felt pure compassion for them, no matter how badly they treated us.

Without any advance warning, Ananta was released from prison after three years. As Adrian's example shows, awakenings — particularly when they are sudden and dramatic — can be difficult to adjust to. It can sometimes take years to integrate them, allowing a shifter to function properly in the everyday world again. And despite her previous knowledge of spirituality — without which the process would probably have been even more difficult — Ananta went through a very challenging phase of adjustment and integration:

I couldn't relate to the world, and people couldn't relate to me. I couldn't even hold conversations with them. When they spoke, I just didn't want to engage in superficial conversation. It sounded like noise. I had no interest. I still had my own way of eating, and people looked at me like there was something wrong with me. My family wanted me to get help.

All my roles had been taken away. When I was deported from Japan and came back to England, I was required to play these roles again, and it was like, "Oh no, I'm not that!" I watched the ego reconstruct itself. There was a real period of confusion that lasted about three years. I didn't know how I was going to play those roles and function in this world.

This was 1997, before nonduality and *satsangs* were a thing in Europe. I couldn't explain what I'd been through to anyone. I didn't know this was awakening. My idea of enlightenment was something different. I didn't think I could be enlightened because I still had feelings and emotions. I thought enlightened people were serene and still.

But in 2000 I went to see a teacher who confirmed that the recognition and the shift had taken place. That confirmation was really important. I started to integrate and to function in the world again. I found that I was able to bring others into direct experience of awakening. But I also found that awakening isn't enough in itself. How do you live in the body-mind? How do you engage in relationships? The issue of integration – the process I'd been through – became a focus of my teaching.

Since then Ananta has been a spiritual guide, working with individuals and groups. Her teaching is based on the discovery she made in a Japanese prison: that in order to wake up, we have to let everything drop away. We have to drop down into our true essence, beyond all roles and attachments. And then we have to integrate this realization into our ordinary lives. Ananta describes the aim of her work as "bringing the simple direct recognition of the realization of our true nature, through all that appears to play in all levels, right back round to the extraordinary ordinariness of life itself. Never the same again and no way back! From here we walk this earth as divine human beings."

"I Choose Joy and Gratitude" – Ed Little's Story

Perhaps the most moving story of transformation through incarceration I have come across is that of Edward Little, a fifty-six-year-old American man who has been in prison in Arkansas since childhood. I was alerted to Ed's story by a man named Lionel Pires, who sent me an email in 2017 after reading my book *The Leap*. He told me that for more than thirty years he had been in contact with an inmate who was sentenced to life without parole at the age of fifteen. Lionel told me, "I realized right away that he had 'woken up' in prison. It is a truly unique perspective in consciousness."

Now semiretired, in the late 1980s Lionel was working as an intake coordinator at a psychiatric hospital in Providence, Rhode Island. At that time, his friend Fred Bohen, a prominent psychiatrist and vice president of Brown University, was serving as a mentor to Edward Little and suggested that Lionel write to him. Lionel and Ed began a correspondence that developed into a close friendship.

Lionel was a spiritual seeker. He had been practicing Transcendental Meditation for several years (and he still practices) and recognized that Ed had undergone some form of spiritual transformation:

> Those who come in contact with Ed realize there is something profoundly different about him in a soul-enlivening way. He is a bit of a legend in prison, to the inmates and guards alike. I feel that consciousness took a child through terrible circumstances and suffering and created a light in the darkest of places. The past thirty-three years of my life have been blessed by Ed.

Ed had a horrific upbringing. His mother was a violent and unstable woman who worked mostly as a bar singer. She shot and killed her husband (not Ed's father) in front of him when he was a toddler and went to prison for four years. During that time Ed and his brother were in foster care. On her release from prison, Ed's mother regained custody of her children. Over the next few years she changed boyfriends and husbands frequently, and Ed and his older brother were shuffled back and forth between the different men. Ed was physically abused by a man who he thought was his father.

During his childhood, the only person Ed felt he could trust was his older brother, who was a drug addict and criminal. It was his older brother who led him into a life of crime. Ed was, in the words of his lawyer Michael Kaiser, speaking at his first parole hearing in 2018, "a screwed-up kid who craved authority and stability, had none and was instead abused and introduced to drugs and violence, and lashed out in impulsive and unfortunate ways."

At the age of fifteen Ed and a sixteen-year-old accomplice held up a store in Little Rock, Arkansas. Ed brandished a gun and shot the store clerk, wounding her. Later a policeman stopped them in their stolen car. As the policeman turned to walk back to his car, Ed and his accomplice decided to make a run for it, and Ed shot at the policeman as they fled. The policeman died. In November 1980, Ed was found guilty of capital murder, aggravated robbery, and first-degree battery. He was spared the death penalty — which at the time would have been the electric chair — because the jury was moved by testimony of a childhood blighted by abuse, neglect, and drug addiction. Instead, he was given a sentence of life without parole.

In the UK and other European countries, Ed probably would have been released from prison many years ago, despite the horrific nature of his crime. In European justice systems, there is a general recognition that crimes — even the most heinous ones — committed by children and adolescents are usually the result of environmental conditioning. In most cases, this means an abusive, violent upbringing in which children are socialized into viewing violence and crime as normal and acceptable. In other words, at least in the vast majority of cases, children and adolescents don't commit murders because they are intrinsically evil (that is, because they are psychopaths or predators) but because they are products of an evil environment.

This would certainly apply to Ed's background, and his crime. According to a psychologist who examined him before his trial, Ed's offense was "the product of transient immaturity rather than intractably bad character, in combination with his association with an older, antisocial peer who likely exerted significant influence over his behavior and his involvement in the crime. The crime had many hallmark features of offenses committed by juveniles: it was impulsive, driven by sensation seeking and reward seeking without consideration of the future consequences of the act, and committed with a peer."

In European justice systems, there is also usually a recognition that such children and adolescents are capable of reform. It is possible for them to become deconditioned so that they learn to see the enormity of their offenses and become able to empathize with their victims. In many cases, they are released from prison under close supervision, sometimes under new identities. But not in Arkansas.

Ed was sixteen years old when he began his sentence. At the time he was small in stature, around five feet tall, and weighed less than 110 pounds. (Even now he weighs only around 135.) He had soft, effeminate features, and as a result was victimized and sexually abused. He was a constant target for sexual attacks and rapes from older inmates. As his lawyer explained at his parole hearing, "Anything you can imagine bad that could happen to someone in prison has happened to Edward, over and over. Simply put, his hard time was much harder than most inmates', as a five-foot-tall child with no ability to defend himself."

During his first decade in prison, Ed committed many disciplinary violations. Most of them were deliberate, as he tried to escape the general population and avoid the constant threat of rape. Eventually Ed learned how to defend himself, starting to fight back when attacked, and the other inmates began to leave him alone. Since that first decade, his disciplinary record has been, as his lawyer put it, "remarkably spare and bereft of serious charges."

Lionel put me in contact with Ed, and I have been corresponding with him over the past year. This book has already shown clearly that transformation through turmoil can occur both suddenly and gradually. Sometimes spiritual awakening is like a gate that is ripped wide open in an explosion, while sometimes it's like a gate that opens so slowly that you're barely aware of its movement.

In Ed's case, his transformation seems to have been both sudden *and* gradual. As with Adrian, Ed's discovery of meditation was the catalyst for his initial transformational experience. This initial transformation lifted him to a higher level of being, which became a platform for further spiritual development:

I have achieved a truly remarkable transformation from the young extremely troubled child I was when I came to prison. It's almost impossible for me to explain to you the place I came from because it was so lost. I was frozen inside without any emotional feelings at all. I wouldn't allow myself to think or feel anything. I was so dysfunctional then that I couldn't understand even remotely the significance of my crime.

Eight years in I began meditating, trying to calm my mind. It was very simple. I would think "in with the good, out with the bad" with my breath, and I would do it every morning and afternoon. It was a very traumatic time for me because the prison was brutal, the inmates and the guards.

One day during a meditation I started crying for the first time I could remember, and it was like a light coming on inside my mind, allowing me to understand what I had done. I cried silently for a long time, trying not to let anyone hear me. I felt so much sorrow for the suffering I had caused and for my family and also for myself. It was that day that transformed me. I started searching for understanding, and so much new information started flowing into my life along with new people. Without the basis for comprehension, I resisted the truths that were before me, so I started the long road putting the pieces together.

One of the main differences for me began when I grasped that life is really about the relationships with other people. That's what gives meaning to our lives. The biggest change in me is empathy. I can now feel someone's joy or feel happy or cry at their pain. I sometimes feel I'm too emotional!

I know that what we put forth into the universe will return. We were made to create, and every thought and action we have is creative. It took me so long to embrace what I know to be reality! It's easy to get caught up in the lives and stories around us. Truths are clearly evident if we just look for them. Life is — I try not to take it anywhere or judge it. I trust my spirit knows how to respond to any situation.

As in so many cases of transformation through turmoil (TTT), an attitude of acceptance was a major factor in Ed's shift. As Lionel describes it, "Horrible tragedy took on new meaning when he totally accepted his situation. Some leap in consciousness allowed him to see that his past experiences no longer defined him." Or as Ed explained to me in more detail:

You have to have acceptance in your life. It's what leads to real change and real peace. You have to first accept yourself and then extend that acceptance to others. I'm so appreciative of the understanding that allowed me to step outside myself and view situations from an unattached perspective. That clarity is truly amazing and doesn't give rise to negative emotions that can cloud our perception.

A lot of other inmates I come into contact with ask me how I remain so positive and happy, and I try to explain that I refuse to allow my surroundings or situation to dictate how I feel or relate to the world around me. I have nothing but compassion for the inmates and guards who live in a world of anger and constant aggression. They can't see that the only person truly affected by their negative energy and emotions is themselves. They perceive life as a dark cloud, never comprehending that it originates from within them. The world is truly within us! I choose joy and gratitude. Appreciation doesn't leave room for negativity in any form.

I feel privileged to have built up a relationship with Ed, and I hope someday to visit him in person. In 2012 the US Supreme Court ruled that life without parole for juveniles was cruel and inhumane. As a result, Ed became eligible for parole at the end of 2018. He is being helped pro bono by his lawyer, Michael Kaiser, who also feels a deep respect for and connection to Ed. To date, Ed has had two unsuccessful parole hearings. Lionel was extremely disappointed that parole was denied, but Ed himself was unconcerned. As Lionel put it, "His state of consciousness and acceptance of what is creates a state of well-being in him that frankly I still find hard to fathom. No victim mentality, no animosity." Or as his lawyer, Michael, told me, "Edward Little exemplifies hope in a hopeless place."

Letting Go

I asked Sam Sutton, director of the Prison Phoenix Trust, why there is such a strong association between prison and spiritual awakening. This was his answer:

It's partly about having time – prisoners may be locked up twenty-three hours a day. So they have a lot of time to reflect and to go into themselves. There's something that happens to longer-term prisoners in particular. Some prisoners, if they're on a short-term sentence, can pretend that life is fine and carry on in the same way. But if you come face-to-face with a ten- or twenty-year sentence, it's not for play. There's a serious gravity. You have to really face yourself and reevaluate your life.

But I think the main thing is that your sense of identity can take a hammering when you're in prison. You lose your old sense of who you are that was provided by your friends, your job, your environment, and all the old habits and patterns of your self — that identity goes up in ashes. It burns up in the fire. And that produces a new kind of identity. That's why we're called the Phoenix Trust. A new identity emerges from the ashes of the old self. That identity is always there, tapping at the door, but sometimes it bursts the door down.

This is an excellent summary of why incarceration holds so much spiritual potential. In fact, Sam highlights the same two factors that I referred to earlier: solitude and inactivity (leading to self-reflection and self-exploration) and the dissolution of psychological attachments (leading to ego-dissolution). Like Sam, I would say that the latter factor is the most significant one. In this chapter, the clearest and most dramatic description of ego-dissolution is probably Ananta's. She was forced to "drop everything" until her old ego-self dissolved away and died. This allowed a new, higher self to emerge inside her.

This applies to cases of TTT in general. Essentially, TTT is about ego-dissolution. In situations of intense stress and turmoil, the ego-self may suddenly give way under the pressure, like a building that collapses in an earthquake. Or it may slowly fall away and eventually disappear through a process of detachment, as psychological attachments are broken down, like a building that collapses after enough individual bricks have been taken away. For some people, both these scenarios may simply lead to a psychological breakdown, but for a minority, the breakdown of the ego heralds a "shift up" to a higher spiritual state. As Sam describes above, a latent awakened self emerges, like a phoenix.

In my view, the emergence of this latent awakened self has massive significance, beyond the impact it has on the shifters themselves. I believe it has *evolutionary* significance, as a part of the unfolding development of living beings on this planet. The unfolding of this awakened self represents the next phase in human evolution — a more intense form of awareness that will one day become normal to all human beings. In this sense, it is the "gnostic being" described by Sri Aurobindo in the last chapter. (I will elaborate on this topic in the final chapter of this book.)

Freedom Is an Inner State

There is no doubt that many people deserve to be in prison. People with incurable personality disorders such as psychopathy or narcissistic personality disorder can't empathize with others and have committed terrible crimes because of their brutality and emotional coldness. But there are also many people who (like Ed Little) have committed crimes due to environmental factors — such as social conditioning, peer pressure, and emotional immaturity — who could be rehabilitated and given the chance to reenter society. (Of course, there are many prisoners who are victims of miscarriages of justice too.) And the point I made in chapter 1 about soldiers applies here too: I find it comforting to think that, out of all the millions of prisoners who are suffering unjustly in terrible conditions, at least a portion of them have undergone — or are undergoing — spiritual awakening.

This applies to prisoners of war and political prisoners too, and to the millions of people who were murdered in concentration camps during the Second World War. As with soldiers, we don't know exactly how common spiritual awakening is in prisoners (this would be another fascinating area of research), but we can safely say that it isn't unusual. So it's likely that there have been many more cases of TTT among prisoners of war and concentration camp inmates than we are aware of. Unfortunately (even with their soul-force providing them with increased resilience and energy) death rates among the inmates of gulags and concentration camps were so high that there were probably many inmates who underwent transformation but didn't survive to tell anyone about it. So again, I find it comforting to think that at least some innocent prisoners had awakening experiences or underwent some form of permanent spiritual transformation.

One of the lessons that the awakenings of prisoners can teach us is that freedom is more than a physical state. Hundreds of millions of human beings — perhaps billions — in the world are physically free but imprisoned by their minds. At least in theory, they are able to live without restrictions, to travel anywhere they like, to meet anybody they want to, and to behave as they wish (so long as they don't break any laws). But their physical freedom doesn't bring them any contentment or fulfillment because they are trapped inside the cage of the ego. They are entangled in patterns of negative thinking, oppressed by anxiety and fear, disturbed by the constant restless turbulence of their thoughts and by their sense of ego isolation. They are encased inside their own minds and bodies, with the rest of reality — including other human beings — out there on the other side of the boundary.

At the same time some prisoners live incredibly restricted lives in a brutal and discordant environment and yet are free: free from anxiety, free from the turbulence of constant thinking, free from separation and duality. They have found an inner well-being that makes the deprivation of their external environment seem meaningless. They have found an inner freedom that makes the restrictions on their outer freedom seem trivial.

Freedom may not always be the blessing that it seems. Sometimes physical freedom actually increases our mental bondage. Too many possibilities and options confuse us. They may dissipate our energies and scatter our attention, since we have too many different things to focus on. Having access to everything we could want, and being able to do anything we want, can make us self-centered, self-indulgent, and ultimately bored with life. When there are so many activities and entertainments in the external world for us to enjoy, we are in danger of losing touch with our own being.

In contrast, restrictions can sometimes be beneficial. When our options are limited, we can focus on the things that truly matter. When the external world is restricted to us — or even closed down altogether — we can turn inside and begin to self-reflect and explore our own being. And as we've seen throughout this chapter, letting go of our attachments in the external world, and living quietly and simply, may allow us to make contact with the deep essence of our being and bring about spiritual awakening.

Of course, monks and nuns have always known this. The monastic way of life is based on the principle that external restrictions can bring inner freedom. And many prisoners have also become aware of this. As one of the letters to the Prison Phoenix Trust expresses it: "All my life I've been lost or so caught up in my own self-centeredness, it's like my whole life I've been in prison. And now I'm actually in prison, I feel so free, so calm, and at ease with life, peace."

4

THE GREATEST LOSS

Transformation through Bereavement

Afamous story in Buddhism is the parable of the mustard seeds. A young woman named Kisa Gotami was grieving the death of her baby son. She carried his body from house to house, pleading for some medicine to bring him back to life. One of her neighbors advised her to go see the Buddha, who asked her to bring him a handful of mustard seeds. The only condition was that, in the Buddha's words, "The mustard seeds must be taken from a house where no one has lost a child, husband, parent, or friend."

Kisa Gotami returned to her village and went from house to house again. But of course, she was unable to collect any mustard seeds, since every family had suffered a bereavement. By the end of the day, the mother realized the impermanence of life and the inevitability of death. As the Buddha expressed it, "The life of mortals in this world is troubled and brief and combined with pain. For there is not any means by which those that have been born can avoid dying.... Not from weeping nor from grieving will anyone obtain peace of mind; on the contrary, his pain will be the greater and his body will suffer."[1]

This parable is so powerful not just because it illustrates the universality of death and bereavement but also because it suggests their transformational effects. Kisa Gotami's acceptance of death transformed her perspective on life. According to the parable, she became a disciple of the Buddha and was his first female follower to attain enlightenment.

Bereavement is the most common type of severe trauma that human beings experience. Most of us have never experienced the trauma of combat or imprisonment, but — as the parable reminds us — every single one of us has experienced the trauma of bereavement. (If you are young this might not be the case, but not for long.) When people die in old age, it seems natural and right. It may even seem like a blessing, if a person has become severely ill or mentally impaired. But when people die before their time, particularly in childhood, it seems incredibly tragic and unjust. Understandably, some people may never recover from the grief of their bereavement and spend the rest of their lives in a state of depression and trauma.

Post-traumatic Growth and Bereavement

Precisely because bereavement is such a traumatic experience, it holds enormous spiritual potential. When a person close to us dies, everything changes radically. Our seemingly stable and orderly lives are thrown into disarray, as if a tidal wave has swept through and washed away every structure. Suddenly the world seems an unfamiliar place, pervaded by emptiness and loss. Our seemingly stable sense of self is broken down. We are no longer sure of who we are, since our identity was bound up with the person we have lost. All our beliefs, hopes, and ambitions seem meaningless and dissolve away.

And it's because bereavement has such a dramatic and powerful effect that, like imprisonment, it is so closely associated with spiritual transformation. We have already seen — for example, in the cases of Adrian Troy and Ed Little in the last chapter — that acceptance is an important factor in TTT. Understandably, many people find the death of loved ones difficult to accept and adjust to (particularly in cases of tragic early death) and so don't move beyond grief into growth and transformation. But when people do acknowledge and accept the death of a loved one, the transformational effect is usually very powerful.

When psychologists began to research post-traumatic growth in the late 1980s, they quickly recognized that bereavement is one of its most significant sources. In one of the first studies of PTG in 1986, the psychologist Stephen Shuchter studied a group of widows and widowers who had lost their partners about two years earlier. Most of them felt that they could see life from a wider perspective, that they were less affected by trivial worries and more appreciative of important things.[2] They felt that they had become more sensitive, more self-reliant, more open, and more spiritual in their everyday lives. Similarly, in a 1998 study of 312 people who had lost loved ones about a year previously, psychologists found that around a third of the group felt more mature and confident in their lives and that they had better communication skills and improved relationships.[3]

Research has shown that these benefits can occur even with the most tragic of deaths, including the loss of children. In a study of bereaved parents, the psychologist Dennis Klass found that, following a period of adjustment and acceptance, many of them felt that their lives had become more authentic and meaningful. Some described a process of spiritual transformation, with an awareness of "connections with that which transcended the physical and biological world, and with their perception of an underlying order in the world."[4] Similarly, in 2002 psychologists studied a group of parents whose children had been murdered. Even in these terrible circumstances, the researchers found that for some people the bereavement had led to profound personal growth, with increased self-reliance, compassion, and inner strength, along with a greater appreciation of life.[5]

Emerging as a Butterfly

In my own research I have also found that bereavement is a major trigger of transformation. In 2012 I interviewed thirty-two people who had transformational experiences caused by intense psychological turmoil (the study was published as a paper called "Transformation through Suffering"). Twenty-four people reported a permanent shift (as opposed to temporary experiences that faded), four of which were related to bereavement. One of the most remarkable cases was a woman named Glyn Hood who lost her daughter following an operation. About two years after her bereavement — and following a whole series of difficulties related to her daughter's death, such as the collapse of her business and financial difficulties — Glyn had a sudden transformational experience in which her old ego dissolved away and a new, higher functioning identity replaced it. She was driving to the supermarket when she became aware that her consciousness was expanding, as if "I had shutters around my brain and they were being pulled up one by one." As she pulled over, knowledge flooded through her mind, and she felt as if she was aware of the essential oneness of everything. Although it took her some time to adjust to it, and to integrate it into her everyday life, this expansive state became Glyn's normal way of being. She told me that it was "like the transformation a caterpillar goes through during the chrysalis stage before emerging as a butterfly."[6]

For my PhD research (which was the basis of my book *The Leap*), I studied twenty-five cases of spiritual awakening, six of which were triggered by bereavement. The most moving case was a man named Graham who lost both his wife and his teenage son in the space of a few months. He felt that he didn't know who he was anymore, having lost his roles as both husband and father. He described how the bereavements had "shattered the thin shell of my ego."[7] But through accepting his predicament and exploring his reactions, he found a deeper sense of identity beneath his ego. He felt a new sense of being present, a more intense awareness of his surroundings, and a greater appreciation of life, and he became less identified with his thoughts and feelings. Eleven years later — at the time I spoke to him — it was clear that Graham had attained a stable, permanent state of wakefulness: "Life has become a lot easier. I'm able to live more in the present moment and value that. Attachments that I had before have been loosed a great deal.... Now everything that comes along is okay. I can say yes to life whatever it brings whereas before I used to have conditions."[8]

In 2017 I decided to conduct a research study specifically on bereavement, to investigate its transformational potential in more detail. Working with my research assistant Krisztina, I interviewed sixteen people who reported a spiritual awakening following bereavement. We also asked the participants to complete two psychometric scales that measure spirituality and wakefulness, to help us ascertain whether they had undergone a transformation.

Our sixteen participants (twelve women and four men) had suffered different forms of bereavement — the death of parents, friends, siblings, and partners or spouses. For one participant, it was an abortion, which she experienced as a painful bereavement. In some cases, the deaths were tragic and violent. There were two murders, three car accidents (also one bicycle accident), a suicide, and a drowning. The other deaths were mainly due to health issues, such as cancer or a heart attack. Most of the deaths were sudden and unexpected. (Bereavements are usually more shocking and traumatic when they are sudden and thus more likely to have an ego-dissolving effect.)

Krisztina and I performed a "thematic analysis" of our interviews (a standard psychological research method) to discover the main aspects of our participants' transformational experiences. A number of changes were reported by almost everyone, such as a less materialistic attitude, a more positive attitude about death (including a sense that death is not the end), a new sense of well-being, and a new appreciation of (and sense of connection to) nature. The participants told us that they had undergone personality changes too, becoming more open, intuitive, authentic, self-loving, and compassionate. They also told us that they had new values and goals in life, such as a stronger desire to help others, to contribute to the world, and to spend more time with loved ones.

All these are common characteristics of wakefulness, shared by all the shifters featured in this book. The participants all scored highly on the scales as well. For most participants, it had been a long time since their transformational experiences (which in most cases had happened at the time of, or shortly after, the bereavements). The average length of time was thirteen years, ranging from three to fifty years. For eight people, it had been more than ten years.

This shows how durable and stable TTT normally is. Once people undergo it, they rarely slip back into their previous state. Sometimes its intensity dims a little as people integrate it into their lives. (We will see this clearly in Renee's story later in this chapter.) But once the higher-functioning awakened self is born, it establishes itself permanently as a person's identity. As one participant of the bereavement study told me, "It feels quietly stable ... like a rewiring has taken place." Or in the words of another, "I can't go back.... You can't unring the bell, or you can't unpop a balloon."[9]

Our research also confirmed that TTT can be both a gradual and a sudden process. Out of the sixteen cases we investigated, there was an even split between gradual and sudden awakening.

"I Feel Connected and Loved and Held" — Suzy's Story

One person we spoke to was a woman in her late fifties named Suzy. More than thirty years ago, when she was a young woman with a six-month-old baby, Suzy's husband was killed in a car accident. Her transformational journey began with an awakening experience at her husband's funeral:

During the first song at his funeral, I had pins and needles in my arms and hands and I was finding it hard to cope. I felt like I was close to collapse. By the second song everything had changed. It felt like some force had come through me to make me strong, and I felt euphoric. Something had shifted in me and I felt powerful and in control. I sang at the top of my voice and at the end thanked everyone for coming. During the wake I laughed and joked with the guests.

However, after the funeral, Suzy's grief returned, and over several days, the pain grew so intense that she contemplated suicide:

I was sitting on the edge of the bed with the pills thinking about suicide, but something told me it was wrong. Something outside of me. I didn't hear anything, no physical voices or anything, but I just knew it was wrong. After that I had a definite feeling that life was precious and that it was a gift. And that's remained ever since.

At that time, Suzy knew nothing about spirituality, but after her husband's death she gradually began a journey of self-exploration, investigating spiritual teachings and cultivating an ongoing state of wakefulness:

Over the past thirty years I've been developing, especially in the last fifteen. My purpose and meaning has been my soul's evolution. Material things don't hold much meaning for me. I try to be the best person I possibly can be. I have profound feelings of connection. Last Tuesday morning I had an immense feeling of, "Oh my God, the universe is working with me, and I feel connected and loved and held."

My husband's death changed my attitude to death. I started to look at death and what death meant. I started to study parapsychology. About four and a half or five years after he died, I came to accept that he had gone on to the next part of this journey. I don't think we're supposed to know what happens when we die. I think that although we're all connected in some way, we're all separate in that we've all got individual journeys.

My husband's death changed my view of what was important in life and what wasn't. I think it jolts you out of stuff that doesn't matter and into stuff that does. You know, things that were important before are more important now. Things like relationships and connections become more important rather than cars and houses and all that stuff.

I feel like it almost gave me a soul, or at least put me in touch with my soul. It opened me up, cracked open a shell.

Nowadays Suzy is a meditation teacher and says, "I absolutely love my work and feel it is my true path in life. I feel whole and complete, although I still have much to learn and feel the need to grow."

"I Choose Love and Not Fear" – Renee's Story

An example of a sudden awakening triggered by bereavement was shared with me by an American woman named Renee. Her story is a good example of how spiritual awakening can remain stable over a long period of time. Renee's shift occurred more than fifty years ago, when she was just fourteen.

An unusual aspect of Renee's awakening is that the person who died wasn't intimately connected to her. While in most cases, transformation through bereavement involves a partner, a close relative, or a friend, in her case it was a boy she was friendly with but not particularly close to. The important factor here is that the pain of bereavement is felt very intensely. This is more likely to happen with the people closest to us but obviously can happen in other cases too:

Danny was this bubbly person, very likable, friendly, funny, mischievous, and I really liked him. When eighth grade ended, I was at home, listening to music, scanning through radio stations, and I happened to come across an announcement that there had been a drowning in my town. It turned out to be Danny. He was diving for golf balls in the river and the current took him under and he drowned.

I was totally devastated, overwhelmed with grief. I couldn't really function. I felt like that for months. I tried everything I could think of to help myself. I tried to write poetry, I tried to write songs, I tried to go to church. But I didn't find any comfort or solace in any of the churches that I went to. I tried to talk to Danny's family, but they were struggling too. Eventually I started walking to the cemetery every Sunday.

I started ninth grade in a total fog. Then one day I was sitting underneath a tree and I looked at the sky and it was as if someone had taken away the veil that was in front of me. I had this intense, overwhelming sense of calm and peace. All the questions I had agonized over for so long were gone. I heard music where there was no music. Colors were vivid in a way I had never seen before.

After that, I was totally accepting of everyone and everything — no judgments, no questions. I had no fear, of anything or anyone. I had this wonderful sense that Danny was with me or that he was causing this to occur. It was quite intense, but I didn't have anyone to talk to about it. My family knew something was happening, but they had no idea what to do, so they didn't do anything. I was in this state for months and months.

Somewhere in the middle of my junior year, I started to notice an odd sensation that something was being pulled away from me. I had a sense that I had been pulled back into reality. It was partly because I became enamored of a boy and because of schoolwork and activities. I could feel this beautiful state of being fading, inching and inching away from me, over weeks and months. When it was finally over, the beautiful intense feelings had modified, but they weren't completely gone. They were just less intense. And they have remained, ever since, at that less intense level.

I still have the ability to look at something and see its beauty, even something that might seem horrific. I still have this sense that every person I meet has something to offer me and that I have something to offer them. I have made a commitment to myself that I simply will not live in fear. I have identified when fear is driving me and when love is driving me, and for the most part I choose love and not fear. Music is still very clear to me, colors are more vivid than ever before. It's like looking at a black-and-white painting and having it colorized in an instant. And you know, I can never go back to really looking at the black and white.

Like many awakened people, at first Renee struggled to make sense of what had happened to her. She tried to interpret her new state in terms of conventional religion. As she told me, "I kept looking at different religions and different belief systems and nothing fit, nothing fit. So I decided one day that no religion or denomination was more true than any other. I decided that I would believe it all. And as soon as I did, I had a framework to understand the world and my own experiences."

Renee's awakening determined the course of her life, forming the values that she has lived by ever since. After school and college, she felt a calling to help relieve other people's suffering and trained as a nurse, eventually spending forty years in the profession. Throughout her life, she has had no attachment to material goods or status symbols. As she told me, "I spent my entire adult life shopping at thrift stores as my primary store. I don't go for fancy things or live in a fancy house. I'd much rather be able to see the world the way I see it than own anything." Renee also feels a deep appreciation for nature and a huge enjoyment of solitude and inactivity:

I look at nature as being the thing that connects me to the universe. I love spending time in nature. I love to lie out on my front porch and listen to the world around me, to hear the birds, the lawnmowers, the people passing, the kids playing. To me that's a form of meditation. Ever since it happened, I have found the world beautiful, found people fascinating. It's made me aware that judgment isn't appropriate, because everything the human race does has a meaning, even if it's horrible. It's given me an appreciation of music and flowers and colors and the arts, and a fabulous profession that I loved and felt a privilege to be part of.

One of the interesting things about Renee's story is her description of how her original wakefulness was first very intense, began to wane, and then stabilized at a lower intensity. As I noted earlier, this is quite a common phenomenon. In his introduction to *The Power of Now*, Eckhart Tolle writes that after his transformation, he lived in "a state of uninterrupted deep peace and bliss" for around five months, and then it "diminished somewhat in intensity" as it became his normal and natural state.[10]

For me, this is one of the more mysterious aspects of awakening. Perhaps it's a part of the adjustment process. It may be that we have to "come down" to some degree in order to regain our normal psychological abilities (like concentration, memory, and rational thinking) so that we can begin to function in the world. But as far as I know, there is no clear explanation for why this deintensification occurs.

Postmortem Contact and Transformation

Following bereavement, many people feel that they continue to have some contact with the person they have lost. Studies show that between a half and three-quarters of bereaved people sense the presence of a deceased loved one.[11] This may just be a feeling that the person is nearby, watching or helping them. It may be a sensory experience of smelling or hearing them — for example, smelling their perfume, being touched by them, or hearing them call out. There are also cases of people receiving communications with the deceased through electronic devices, such as computers, radios, or telephones. Most dramatically, many people report actually seeing their deceased loved ones. Sometimes they see a deceased person lying in bed, sitting in an armchair, or walking into the room. These experiences may continue for many months after a person's death, sometimes indefinitely. In other cases, they are isolated occurrences.

One variant of these experiences is when people see relatives or friends around the time of their death. In most of these cases, people have no idea that the friend or relative has died and find out only afterward. A friend of mine woke up suddenly in the middle of the night and saw her grandmother standing at the foot of her bed. "Grandma, what are you doing here?" my friend asked, confused. "Why aren't you at home in bed?" Her grandmother said nothing and disappeared after a few seconds. The next morning, my friend received a phone call with the news that her grandmother had died during the night.

A few months after our research project was completed, a woman named Mirtha wrote to me to share a transformational experience she had after the death of her son. Her son died in a plane crash, just three months before he was due to get married. Four nights before his death, while awake in the middle of the night, Mirtha had a vision of a monarch butterfly flying and then falling to the ground. Two days after the accident, she "suddenly realized (without any thought or analysis) that the vision was the exact replica of my son's accident, in a symbolic way."

This helped her to understand that there was a meaning to her son's death. Over the next one and a half years, whenever Mirtha felt an intense longing for her son, a monarch butterfly would appear shortly afterward — sometimes as a real butterfly flying by or sometimes as an image in a book, in a shop window, or on a computer screen. This convinced her that her son was still alive in some form and helped her to shift into a state of acceptance.

In fact, Mirtha's transformational experience is a wonderful example of how an attitude of acknowledgment and acceptance can facilitate TTT. With great courage, she made a conscious attempt to face up to — and even explore — her mental turmoil:

> In the middle of the turmoil, I was invaded by an inexplicable sense of peace. I knew it was because I had just surrendered. This peace has not left me since then. It has increased, actually, as it has led me to a much deeper spiritual life. I think it is important to feel the pain as raw as it is. It is necessary for healing. I never took any pills to dull it.
>
> I know that the last thing my son would have wanted for me, his mother, is to see me lying on a bed, blaming life, God, the universe, the Higher Self, or whoever for what had happened. On the contrary, I just have a feeling of gratefulness for the gift of having had him in my life for thirty-seven incredible years.

"I Feel Like I Have Somebody on the Other Side" – LeeAnn's Story

In our research we didn't directly ask the participants whether they had sensed the presence of the deceased person. But one person who described this as an important aspect of her transformation was an American woman named LeeAnn.

LeeAnn was forty-six when I talked to her. Three years earlier, her close friend Bruno was murdered while working as a nightclub bouncer. Bruno was shot when he intervened with a gang member who was intending to shoot a member of a rival gang. LeeAnn's grief became especially intense when the case went to trial. She was close to Bruno's family and stayed with them during the trial. There was video footage of the murder, which understandably none of the family wanted to watch. But LeeAnn somehow felt compelled to watch it. She found the footage intensely traumatic and felt exhausted for days afterward.

LeeAnn's transformational experience occurred shortly after the trial, on New Year's Eve, which she spent with her roommate:

We decided we were going to stay in for New Year's Eve, so I said, "Let's just relax, like let's just chill out and just see what happens." At about eight o'clock we had this experience. My roommate was on the chair and I was on the couch. The energy in the room just started changing on its own. There was no alcohol, no substance, no marijuana, no anything involved in this. We were completely sober and in a normal state of mind.

Our ceiling fan light flickered. The light started changing, and then all of a sudden, it was as if we were washed in gold. It wasn't normal, but it was real. It was happening. I thought, "Am I having a stroke?" But my roommate was having the same experience. The room filled with this golden light. There was a sense of peace that was overwhelming. I didn't even know anything so peaceful and beautiful could exist. It was bliss.

Now the experience becomes a little sketchy because so much happened. First, I started going through every memory I ever had in my life. I was taken on the journey of my whole life in milliseconds. I don't know how I absorbed all the information. I experienced crazy emotions, and all the past thoughts of my life. And then it seemed like I was pushed back into my body, if that makes any sense. It was as if all my memories were pulled out of me and then I was pushed back in.

And then I saw Bruno in his human form. My eyes were closed, but he was standing there, surrounded by blue colors and light. He said to me, "You keep asking for me to come back. Don't ask that – this is where I'm supposed to be." There weren't a lot of words – just, "This is where I'm supposed to be. I don't want to come back. Everything will be okay."

Then it was as if Bruno plugged me into something, some kind of energetic field. It didn't scare me. Afterward I felt an amazing sense of wholeness, but at the same time I felt shaken. There was a lot of crying. My roommate had the same kind of experience and the same reactions. It lasted for about thirty minutes and ended when someone else came in.

The next day I didn't really speak. I didn't have anything to say. I was just really trying to process what I'd just experienced.

And suddenly it was as if all the hurt and the pain disappeared. And I was sitting there and heard Bruno speak to me. It was Friday night, about nine o'clock, and he told me that he wanted me to text his brother. I didn't want to do it – his brother was in a terrible state, and I didn't want to tell him that I had had contact with Bruno. They were a Mormon family, and I didn't know how they would react. So I was arguing with Bruno aloud, telling him I didn't want to do it. But Bruno kept saying to me, "No, I need you to do that, I need you to text my brother, and this is what I want you to text." So I sent the text. And Bruno's brother replied straightaway. He was working on a car that day and was sure Bruno was with him. He said, "There's absolutely no way that I was alone today. There were moments when I needed two people to do the work, and he was there with me, helping. It felt so effortless."

From that point forward, everything in my life has changed. Prior to that I was in this bubble, kind of sealed off with nowhere else to go. I wasn't seeking anything. Nothing was pushing me to find anything. Now I feel like I'm in the womb and there's this little veil that I can see through. I can see that there's another world and the veil is thinning. I can feel more of what's out there.

Bruno has been audible to me from that day forward. He has stayed with me. At that point he opened something up for me. I feel like I have somebody on the other side of wherever we are. It's opened up my heart, my mind, my spirit, my energetic connection, the way I feel about everybody, everything.

At the time I spoke to LeeAnn, she was still adjusting to her shift and struggling with the concept of time. In particular, she found it difficult to recall memories or to judge how long ago past events occurred. Living in the Deep South of the United States, she was surrounded by fundamentalist religious people who she felt wouldn't understand her, so she rarely talked about her transformation. Nevertheless, LeeAnn feels exhilarated by the new world that has opened up to her and is amazed by the changes she has undergone.

One of the biggest changes is that LeeAnn is no longer afraid of death. As she told me, "My biggest fear was death. But I don't see it as death anymore. I just see it as a transition to something else, something greater." Another change is that now she spends a lot of time in quietness. Before she was a sociable and extroverted person who constantly needed other people's company, but now she relishes silence and solitude. As she told me, "Sometimes I can sit in silence for the whole weekend, which I would have never been able to do before, ever. Now I need silence. I want it."

Similarly, before Bruno's death, LeeAnn never felt any special connection to or interest in nature. As she put it, "I wasn't an outdoors person at all." But now she spends a lot of time in nature and feels a strong empathic connection to animals. She feels the same sense of connection to other people, with a strong desire to help them:

> It's all about the interaction for me. The only thing that I think has any value is the present moment and the person I'm connecting to. I started seeing every single person as myself. I have a feeling of connection to everything, whether or not it's living. If I walk into a store, if I'm walking down the street, if I'm talking, I have to have eye contact with the person. I have to connect.

LeeAnn was never especially materialistic before her transformation, but now she feels a strong aversion to the idea of buying unnecessary things or making money just for the sake of it. Like Renee, she has stopped buying new things, using thrift stores instead. She feels uneasy throwing anything away.

LeeAnn has the same job she had before her transformation, as a director of practice relations for a dermatology group. Initially she struggled with some aspects of the job but adapted by changing her attitude. Now she focuses on the well-being of patients and other staff members rather than thinking in terms of profit. As she told me, "I want to make sure that every patient that walks through the door, every employee that works there, they're always respected, valued, cared about — it's ridiculously important to me."

When I asked LeeAnn to summarize the main aspects of her shift, she returned to the analogy of breaking out from a limited perspective:

> I'll give you a picture. Before I was like a square or rectangle, linear and boxed in. I was in a box. And now the next picture is fluid and circular and energetic and golden. It's not without its turbulence, but the turbulence is almost good because I know that it's going somewhere else. If you're in a box, you know you can't go any further. You do what you have to do, and that's it. And because I was in a box, I felt trapped. I'd become frustrated, angry, irritated, full of my own problems and worries. Even though I think I was empathetic, there was a lot that I was doing just for me.
>
> Now I'm out of the box and floating in these waters, in this energy, and I feel that the tides are going to bump me into the people I'm supposed to have contact with. I feel like there's a reason for everything. I don't need to know the answers. I don't need labels. I don't need to know what happens at the end. I have a sense of peace that's telling me there's a bigger purpose, a bigger mission, and we're all part of the same mission. I just need to stay involved in my purpose, and everything will work out.
>
> I feel a tremendous amount of love and a tremendous amount of support. I have a tremendous amount of gratitude.

For LeeAnn, everything goes back to the golden light she experienced on New Year's Eve, when she encountered Bruno again. She can feel the light inside her and feels as if she is sharing it with other people as she interacts with them. The main reason she feels negatively toward material things is that, as she says, "the more things we have, the further away we are from our source. You can think of the source in different ways, but for me it's the golden light."

Transformation in History

For those who live in more affluent parts of the world, it is no longer common for children to die during infancy. But before the twentieth century, infant and youth mortality rates were incredibly high. One study of forty-three historical cultures — including ancient Rome, medieval Japan, imperial China, and Renaissance Europe — found that a quarter of all babies died during their first year, and almost half of all children died before the age of fifteen.[12] These figures were remarkably consistent across all cultures. This means that it would have been rare for any parents not to experience the death of at least one child.

Looking back, we might assume that parents viewed the death of children as an inevitable part of life and weren't as devastated as modern parents in the same situation. We might assume that our ancestors protected themselves by not allowing themselves to become as emotionally attached to their children as we do. But I doubt this was the case. I think it's highly likely that our ancestors were as grief-stricken and traumatized by the loss of their children as we would be. And because the death of children was so common, I can imagine many of our ancestors living in a permanent state of grief, numbed and dazed by the trauma of losing their children. Perhaps this explains why so many of our ancestors were religious. Even though it must have confused them (and perhaps also angered them) that a supposedly benevolent God could allow their children to die, their religion must have helped them find meaning in their suffering, partly through the belief in an afterlife where they might see their children again.

Recently I found a tragic example of the trauma of parental bereavement in a biography of one of my favorite poets, William Wordsworth. He is most famous for poems like "Tintern Abbey" and "Intimations of Immortality," which describe a spiritual force pervading the natural world, as well as poems describing the beauty of the wild landscapes of his home region, the Lake District of Northern England. Born in 1770, Wordsworth knew nothing about Eastern spiritual traditions (or even mystical Christianity), but it is clear that he was a very spiritually developed person.

I didn't know much about Wordsworth's life and was sad to learn that it was tragically blighted by bereavement — in particular, by the death of his children. In 1812 (at a time when he was still distraught over the death of his brother a few years earlier) two of Wordsworth's five children died. First it was his daughter Catherine, who had suffered ill health since birth and wasn't expected to survive into adulthood. Then it was his six-year-old son, Thomas, who died of pneumonia after contracting measles. (The three other children became seriously ill with measles, and their lives hung in the balance for days.)

Both Wordsworth and his wife were in a deep state of grief for years afterward. As he wrote movingly to a friend soon after the death of his son, "I dare not say in what state of mind I am; I loved the Boy with the utmost love of which my soul is capable, and he is taken from me — yet in the agony of my spirit in surrendering such a treasure I feel a thousand times richer than if I had never possessed it."[13] Three years later Wordsworth wrote a beautiful but intensely sad short poem called "Surprised by Joy" about the "most grievous loss" of his daughter. He described the pain of knowing that "my heart's best treasure was no more" and that nothing "could to my sight that heavenly face restore."

Wordsworth's reaction to his children's deaths was no doubt typical and illustrates the heavy weight of trauma that our ancestors had to carry. Unfortunately, Wordsworth doesn't seem to have experienced any spiritual growth after his bereavements.[14] However, I find it a comforting thought that, out of all the hundreds of millions of our ancestors who suffered the tragedy of the death of young children, at least a portion of them must have undergone TTT. I have made the same point about prisoners and soldiers in previous chapters, but in the case of bereavement, the point is even more relevant, since the loss of a child was a much more common experience than imprisonment or war.

I firmly believe that there are many more spiritually awakened people around us than we realize — people who have undergone TTT but have no background in spirituality and so don't fully understand what's happened to them and haven't talked to anyone about it. And this was no doubt true of previous generations. Throughout previous centuries, in different cultures all around the world, there have surely been millions of unknown spiritually awakened people whose awakening was triggered by hardship and trauma — and probably most commonly by the loss of children.

5

WAKING UP TO LIFE THROUGH DEATH

Transformation through Facing Death

In 2018 I was invited to speak at a conference near Los Angeles and was excited to find that one of my fellow speakers was the author Mark Nepo. I was looking forward to meeting Mark, partly because he is a poet (like me) but also because I knew that he had undergone a powerful experience of transformation through turmoil.

I liked Mark straightaway, and we spent a lot of time together over the three-day conference. Some authors — even spiritual ones! — can have an air of self-importance about them, but Mark is humble and unpretentious. He has the calm presence of someone who knows what is important and what isn't and who feels grateful to be alive and for every experience that constitutes life. His poems and other writings flow from a place of deep spiritual insight and wisdom.

Mark reached this place through terrible, life-opening suffering. In his thirties he was diagnosed with a rare form of cancer — a lymphoma between his brain and skull — which brought him close to death. At first he felt broken down, terrified at the prospect of the pain and suffering that lay ahead and at the prospect of dying so young. But eventually this changed. In Mark's words, "By facing what I was given as authentically as possible, I was given access to the well of all being. This common authority of being lifted me with reserves of resilience whose existence I had never suspected."

A new stronger and deeper identity emerged inside Mark, like a phoenix. It has now been more than thirty years since his recovery, but the lessons he learned through his suffering and treatment still remain clear and urgent.

"It changed everything," he told me at the conference. "Even now when I wake up in the morning, I still feel like life and death are perched over my shoulders. Even now I'm simply glad to wake up and be here. I literally became a different person. It taught me everything I now know. It was like going through a gate. You look back and then the gate you have come through has disappeared, and you know there is no going back. And having left that gate, the world is a completely different place."

Death, the Great Awakener

If the experience of bereavement — the death of people who are close to us — can bring about spiritual awakening, it's not surprising that encountering our *own* death can bring about transformation too. We've already looked at some examples in the first three chapters in relation to the transformational experiences of soldiers and prisoners. Certainly, in the cases of David and Gary in chapter 1, their encounters with death as soldiers (witnessing the deaths of colleagues and being exposed to the danger of dying themselves) were a significant aspect of their transformation. In chapter 2, I described the awakening experience of the author Arthur Koestler, which occurred when he was in prison waiting to be executed. Also in that chapter, I discussed how the threat of death was most likely a factor in the transformations of the gulag inmates.

In this chapter, however, we will focus on encounters with death outside the context of unusual situations such as war or incarceration. For convenience's sake, I will make a distinction between two different types of encounters with death.

On the one hand, we will look at what researchers call near-death experiences (NDEs). NDEs may occur when a person is either very close to death (such as during a fall or in a coma) or actually dead in a clinical sense. After cardiac arrest, for instance, a person's brain and body may shut down for a short period before they are resuscitated. In many cases, people report that even though their brain showed no signs of activity, they continued to be conscious and underwent a remarkable series of experiences.

Typically, in NDEs people report a feeling of leaving their body and looking down at it from above, then floating away into space. They feel a tremendous sense of well-being, with feelings of connectedness and love. Sometimes they encounter deceased relatives or beings of light. They may also, though less frequently, see a review of their whole lives, flashing by in the space of a few seconds. (LeeAnn described this in the last chapter, although not in the context of an NDE.) Although they may last only for a few seconds of normal time, NDEs usually have a powerful transformational effect.

However, encounters with death can lead to spiritual awakening even if a person doesn't specifically have an NDE. This is the second type of death encounter we will look at: when people encounter death through a sudden accident or injury or through a long-term illness such as cancer. As Mark Nepo found, even without an NDE, becoming aware of the reality and inevitability of death — and the fragility and temporariness of life — can bring about a major shift.

I will look at this second type of experience first. To make a distinction from NDEs, I will call this type of experience an intense mortality encounter (or IME, for short).

Intense Mortality Encounters

As with bereavement, a great deal of research shows that IMEs can lead to post-traumatic growth. A wide range of life-threatening experiences are associated with PTG, including natural disasters, accidents, and chronic illness.

One of the earliest studies to identify the phenomenon of PTG was a study of the survivors of a ferry disaster. On March 6, 1987, a ferry traveling from England to Belgium capsized, causing the death of 193 people. In the months after the disaster, many of the survivors (around three hundred people) suffered symptoms of post-traumatic stress disorder, including upsetting dreams, anxiety, emotional detachment and numbness, and difficulties with sleep and concentration.

Three years later, the psychologist Stephen Joseph, then a PhD student, conducted a survey of the survivors and found some surprising results. Although PTSD was still common (albeit with diminished symptoms), Joseph found that 43 percent of the survivors reported that "their view of life had changed for the better."[1] They reported that they no longer took life for granted, that they valued their relationships more, that they lived each day to the full, and that they felt more experienced about life and so on. (Interestingly, researchers have estimated that 47 percent of people undergo PTG in the aftermath of any trauma, which is close to the 43 percent figure in this study.)

There is also a lot of evidence that intense mortality encounters can lead to transformation through turmoil. As mentioned earlier in the book, it is difficult to draw the line between PTG and TTT — in fact, there is no line, just a gradual intensification of experience. All of the characteristics of PTG (such as appreciation, authenticity, a sense of meaning and purpose) occur in TTT too, but in a more intense form. And because TTT is more intense overall, new characteristics emerge with the increasing intensity, such as a sense of connection and oneness, a feeling of bliss, and an awareness of an underlying spiritual force.

One difference between PTG and TTT is that the former is almost always a gradual process, whereas we have seen that TTT can be both gradual *and* sudden. Some types of trauma seem to be more associated with either gradual or sudden TTT. For example, bereavement seems to be especially likely to lead to gradual TTT. (As we saw in the last chapter, in my study of TTT through bereavement, the cases were equally split between gradual and sudden.) On the other hand, intense mortality encounters seem to be especially likely to bring about *sudden* TTT. This is particularly the case when they occur in the form of a single, isolated encounter, caused by an accident or the sudden onset of a temporary health condition.

In my book *Out of the Darkness*, I told the story of Tony, a man from my home city of Manchester, England, who had a heart attack at the age of fifty-two, at a time when he was a successful business-man, working around sixty hours a week. After his recovery, Tony felt as if he had woken up out of a dream. All of a sudden, he was aware of the value of things that he had always taken for granted, such as the people in his life, the natural things around him, and the fact of being alive itself. The goals he had previously lived for — such as money, success, and status — seemed unimportant. He felt an inner joy and a sense of connection to nature and other people that he had never known before.

As a result of this transformation, Tony decided to sell his busi-ness and to use part of the money to buy a launderette. In my local area he was known as the "launderette guru" because he used to tell his customers about his transformation and remind them not to take anything in their lives for granted. One afternoon while I was waiting for my clothes to be washed, he told me, "I know what it means to be alive, how wonderful it is. And I want to share that with as many other people as I can."

Another example of TTT brought about by an intense mortality encounter was shared by a Scottish journalist named Emma Cowing. In 2008 Emma was reporting from the front line of the conflict in Afghanistan, when she collapsed from acute heatstroke. Her heart stopped beating for four minutes, and she was in a coma for eighteen hours. She suffered a heart attack and complete liver and respiratory failure. Her life was saved by army medics, and she was airlifted to a hospital in the UK for further treatment. She recovered so quickly that, amazingly, she was released after just six days.

As she left the hospital, arm in arm with her father, Emma was confronted with the kind of urban scene that previously would have seemed drab and ugly. But now it seemed beautiful: "It was starting to rain. Cars were beeping on the nearby dual carriageway. The smell of cut grass mingled with that of an overflowing bin on which a seagull was solemnly picking at a kebab. I thought it was wonderful.... I found myself standing in awe."[2]

In an article written five years after the experience, Emma described how she now felt a strong sense of gratitude for life and a sense of awe at the "small things" she rarely paid attention to before. As she described it, "The mundane seems suddenly wonderful.... You learn to savor what you have and not yearn, as you once did, for what you don't have." She also described a sense of delight in "those little moments that sneak by before you even notice them.... The things which make us happiest can also be the easiest."[3]

I contacted Emma to find out if — seven years after the article and twelve years after the experience itself — she had retained this perspective. This is what she told me:

Yes, it has stayed with me. My whole life has been framed by what happened twelve years ago. It has crystallized as my life has moved on. It's allowed me to reframe things in a positive way. I could be having a really bad day, and then I remember that I almost didn't have a today. I just look up at that lovely blue sky up there. Every day is a bonus, no matter what happens in it. So I'm a much more relaxed person than before. I don't sweat the small stuff much now. Whatever happens, it's never going to be as bad as what happened to me in Afghanistan.

I do think that what I went through has made me more resilient. When it comes to the big stuff I've faced since – losing my dad, losing my best friend, being made redundant, the current pandemic situation, and so on – I feel far more equipped to tackle them, stay strong, and not fall apart. I think that having been through that one singular experience twelve years ago, I know now that I can cope with anything. One way or another, I'll get out the other side.

I still have that childlike sense of wonder. Even if life is busy and stressful, there are always spaces for joy and wonder, in every day. It's about learning to recognize those spaces.

The experience didn't lead to major changes in the way I live. I didn't start a new career or give everything away to a charity. But it changed my outlook, definitely. It was about learning to cherish life, to appreciate the small and simple things that make up life, including my relationships. It was about finding joy.

Cancer

In a sense, people like Emma and Tony who undergo a shift after an isolated encounter with death are the most fortunate ones. Their IMEs were sudden and brief but transformed them permanently. After exposure to the threat of death, they regained their health, retaining their heightened awareness for the rest of their lives.

When people are diagnosed with cancer, the threat of death is, of course, an ongoing one. Death hovers over them continually for months or years. Cancer also causes ongoing pain and discomfort, which is often exacerbated by treatment such as chemotherapy. As a result, cancer is often a terrible experience of intense, protracted suffering. But precisely *because* of this, cancer has a great deal of spiritual potential.

Again, research has shown a strong association between cancer and PTG. In fact, cancer seems to be more strongly associated with PTG than any other illness. One psychologist, Ruthanne Kastner, coined the term *thriving* for the experience of breast cancer patients who reported that they were living more authentically, with a stronger sense of responsibility, a more accepting attitude to death, and a stronger spiritual sensibility.[4] Other studies have highlighted improved relationships, increased self-confidence, and higher levels of spirituality and appreciation for life in cancer patients.[5]

I wrote about a number of cases of TTT in relation to cancer in *Out of the Darkness*, so I won't investigate this area in detail here. But I'd like to mention a few examples I have come across since writing that book.

One example comes from a friend of mine, Jane Metcalfe, who was diagnosed with cervical cancer in her early forties. It happened at a time when she was living a very hectic life and had a turbulent relationship with her partner. The diagnosis prompted her to reevaluate her life. Illustrating how an IME — and intense psychological turmoil in general — can dissolve away psychological attachments and break down the ego, she told me:

> I was told over the phone that I had stage 2 cancer of the cervix. It had a kind of dismantling effect on me. Immediately after I put the phone down, I thought, "Cancer. Why me?" Then, in the next instant, "Why not me?" In a split second I had a complete turnaround: I knew that the woman I identified with, who rushed back and forth to London from the south coast for singing and teaching work, while juggling life with a young child and a difficult partner, wasn't "me." I saw my life spinning, the threads swirling wildly around in some kind of spool, then I saw another image of me as a lemming running with the herd at full tilt toward the edge of a cliff. What I saw, however bizarre, was an apt representation of my life.
>
> But now a much bigger part of me stepped forward. And with that recognition my lemming self screeched to a halt and turned

against the herd. I was immediately imbued with a new energy. Instead of feeling numb, I felt vibrantly and boundlessly alive.

From this point on, Jane lived more quietly and slowly, following her intuition rather than the demands of her ego-mind. Her cancer went into remission, which she was sure was due to her new sense of authenticity and self-attunement. She left her partner and put her career on hold, beginning a journey of self-exploration that has continued to this day. She told me, "What the diagnosis of cancer triggered was the emergence of a whole, bright, true Self that had been glimpsed, though largely ignored, for years. It was only when I trusted it to run the whole show that things changed irrevocably."

Jane's story highlights one of the strange aspects of cancer and TTT: in some cases, transformation occurs *immediately* after a diagnosis of cancer, without any period of adjustment or acceptance. It seems paradoxical that a shift into a state of freedom and joy should occur straight after a person is told that they are seriously ill and in danger of dying, but there are many cases of people reacting in this way. The best example I referred to in *Out of the Darkness* was Irene, who woke up to a different world the morning after she was diagnosed with breast cancer. She felt an intense feeling of gratitude for life and a heightened awareness of her surroundings. She recalled that she could see "an energy radiating from the trees" and felt "a tremendous feeling of connectedness."[6]

Irene's cancer went into remission after a few months but returned thirteen years later, leading to her death (after the publication of *Out of the Darkness*). I was in contact with her not long before she died. She felt immensely grateful to have spent those thirteen years in a state of heightened awareness and appreciation. Even though her life was short by modern standards — she was in her early fifties when she died — she felt privileged to have lived so intensely and fully.[7]

On the day I was planning to write this chapter, I heard the sad news that the Indian film actor Irrfan Khan (star of *Slumdog Millionaire* and *Life of Pi*, among many other films) had died. He was fifty-three years old and had been suffering from cancer for the past two years. It was a strange and sad coincidence because I was already planning to write about him in this chapter. Shortly after his diagnosis, on being told that he may have a limited amount of time left to live, Irrfan gave an interview in which he described how his attitude to life had shifted since his diagnosis:

> It has put me in a rapture state.... I would have never reached that state even if I had done meditation for thirty years.... But this sudden jolt has put me into a platform where I could look at things in a completely different manner. And for that I am really thankful.
>
> There's no guarantee of life with anybody. My mind could always tell me to hang a kind of chip on your neck and say, "I have this disease and I could die in a few months or a year or two." Or I could just avoid this conversation completely and live my life the way it offers me. And it offers so much. I admit I was walking around with blinders. I couldn't see what it offered me.... Clarity came like lightning. You stop your contemplation, you stop your planning, you stop the noise. You see the other aspect of it. It gives you so much. Life offers you so much. That's why I feel like I have no other words but thanks. There are no other words, there's no other demand, there's no other prayer.[8]

With cases such as Irrfan's and Irene's, we have to let go of the assumption that dying must be a distressing and traumatic experience. Even when a person dies at a relatively early age, with their full potential unfulfilled, they may still leave this world in a state of ease and acceptance.

Our attitude to death depends on our state of consciousness. In an egocentric mode, we are afraid of death. When death is imminent, we feel anxiety, bitterness, and regret. Death seems tragic because it takes away everything we have accumulated and everything we are attached to. When we place ourselves at the center of the universe, our own death means the end of the whole universe.

But once a person has undergone spiritual awakening, there is little or no fear of death. In fact, awakened people usually sense that there is some form of life after death. They sense a spiritual essence inside them that seems to transcend the body and won't be extinguished when their body and brain stop functioning. In addition, since awakened people don't perceive themselves as the center of the universe, they know their personal existence is not the be-all and end-all. They know that the world and the human race will continue without them, and that in some sense the essence of their being will continue to express itself through other human beings and other life-forms. Awakened people may not *want* to die, because they feel they have more to contribute to the world or more creative or spiritual potential to fulfill. But if death comes, they will accept it without fear or regret.

This is clearly what happened to Irene and Irrfan. Their diagnoses of cancer triggered a spiritual awakening, which enabled them to face death with peace and equanimity.

Near-Death Experiences

Imagine if you had an IME like Emma or Tony and, *in addition*, you had an experience of leaving your body, traveling through space toward a soft translucent light, perhaps meeting beings of light and/or deceased relatives, all with a feeling of intense joy and peace — in other words, a near-death experience. While the spiritual potential of any IME is fairly high, the spiritual potential of an NDE is higher still. In fact, NDEs probably have the most spiritual potential of any *single* experience (as opposed to longer-term situations of suffering, such as imprisonment or bereavement) that human beings can undergo.

While only a small portion of people undergo awakening through IMEs, it's unusual for people *not* to undergo some degree of awakening after NDEs. If they don't, it's usually because the experience conflicts too radically with their view of reality, and so they resist and suppress it. NDEs are certainly difficult to make sense of in terms of the materialistic paradigm of our culture, so people are often confused by them, at least initially. One study found that 57 percent of people were afraid to talk about their NDEs and that 27 percent didn't tell anyone about them for more than a year afterward.[9] However, in most cases, people who initially suppress an NDE eventually go through a process of acceptance and integration. And once they do, the experience transforms them fundamentally.

Studies have repeatedly shown that after NDEs people undergo a major shift in perspective and values. They become less materialistic and more altruistic; they feel more connected to and appreciative of nature, with a heightened sense of love and compassion for other people. Their perception of their surroundings becomes more vivid, with a heightened sense of beauty. Some people even report developing psychic abilities. They often begin to relish solitude and inactivity in a way that they had never done before. It's as if, after spending their previous lives in a constant state of doing, they begin to live in a state of *being*. In the words of the Dutch NDE researcher Pim van Lommel, "The long-lasting transformational effects of an experience that lasts only a few minutes was a surprising and unexpected finding."[10]

Since all the characteristics I've mentioned above are characteristics of wakefulness, this is another way of saying that NDEs often bring about spiritual awakening.

I've never done research specifically on near-death experiences, but in my general research on spiritual awakening and TTT, I have come across several remarkable examples. Below I share two of the most powerful NDE stories I have encountered.

"It Has Made My Life Much More Interesting" – David Ditchfield's Story

At the age of forty, David Ditchfield was an unsuccessful musician who felt a strong sense of failure and frustration in every aspect of his life. As he told me, he was "chasing after the wrong kind of goals" and felt like a misfit. Even in his relationships, he felt that he'd been "chasing after the wrong type of girls" whom he wasn't suited to. He didn't have any academic qualifications and had spent many years doing dreary manual work, which he felt he wasn't cut out for. He felt unfulfilled and ungrounded, and he drank heavily to try to fill the void and to overcome his insecurity about not fitting in.

David knew nothing about spirituality or near-death experiences. His only encounter with the esoteric world was when he tagged along with two friends to see a demonstration by a medium. During the event, the medium singled him out and told him that his life was about to change in a huge way.

A few months later, the medium's prediction came true. David was seeing off a friend at a train station near Cambridge. He stepped onto the train to help his friend with her luggage and hug her good-bye, but as he stepped back off, his long coat got stuck in the train's closing doors. Unable to take off the coat, he found himself trapped as the train set off. He was pulled along the platform as the train gathered speed, being "tossed around like a rag doll." Then he was sucked into the gap between the train and the platform and ended up on the train track, with the train hurtling by above him.

Despite the danger, David felt strangely calm. To maximize his chances of survival, he pushed himself as far down into the track as he could. The final carriage passed over him, and he felt a surge of joy, realizing that he had survived. But now he came aware of a sharp pain. He noticed that the left sleeve of his coat had been ripped to shreds, then saw that his arm had been severed from the elbow down. But rather than feel any shock or panic, he told himself with a sense of detachment, "That's the inside of my arm!" and looked curiously at the nerves and veins and muscles. Surveillance footage showed that just thirteen seconds elapsed from the moment the train started moving to when it passed over David's body. But for him time expanded massively. Those thirteen seconds seemed like hours. As he told me, "Everything unfolded in a slow, dreamlike way. I felt an unearthly, absolute sense of calmness."

David's friend Anna saw the accident and pressed the train alarm. Once the train came to a standstill, she announced that she wanted to say a prayer for him. A woman sitting nearby said that she was a Christian and offered to lead the prayers. All the passengers in the carriage prayed together, and David says that he "felt the energy of their prayers. Somehow I sensed that I was being supported and the energy was helping me to stay calm."

David was rushed to the hospital by paramedics, with his life hanging in the balance, since he was losing so much blood. Shortly after arriving at the hospital, he lost normal consciousness. Suddenly he found himself in a completely different environment, immersed in a darkness that seemed warm and soft, with vivid colors and lights around him. His pain had disappeared, and he felt very tranquil. David told me:

I could see pulsating colors like little orbs, much brighter and sharper than any colors I'd seen in normal life. Watching them was really relaxing and therapeutic. It was such a beautiful place, with a feeling that I was being cared for and supported. I thought that this is what it must be like to die – and then wondered if it meant that I had just died.

The next thing I realized was that I was lying on a big slate, almost like a medieval altar. It was hard but very comfortable. I assumed I was in a room of some kind. Across my body all the wounds were completely healed. My arm was intact, with no bruises, no scars or blood. Then I looked up and saw three white grids of pure white light shining into my eyes. I couldn't take my eyes off them. Although the light was so bright, it didn't hurt my eyes at all.

Then suddenly I was aware of a being at my feet — a being of light that was neither male nor female, with pure white skin and blond hair. It stared at me with a knowing smile, and I felt that somehow it had known me all my life, as if it was my soul mate. I felt immense comfort radiating from it. I laid my head back and realized that there were two other beings around me who were also radiating a sensation of unconditional love. They were more feminine, with warmer and darker skin, similar to Native Americans. I felt like I was being prepared for something but didn't know what. The beings began to spread their hands over different parts of my body, as if they were healing me with a strange, powerful energy. The feeling of love was overwhelming, immersing my whole body. I felt like my soul was being healed. It was as if all the feelings of love you've had throughout your whole life, from your mother or pet cat and your partners, were condensed into the beings' hands.

The sensation of love became stronger, and as I looked at my feet, I saw a huge tunnel of light drawing toward me. I felt — and I still believe this now — that the white light was the source of all creation. I never dreamed I would ever see anything so beautiful. Like the grids I'd seen before, it was blindingly bright but didn't hurt my eyes. It was the beginning, where the universe started. It was surrounded by swirling flames of yellow and red and green, and the colors were transforming into white light at the center. It was the light of pure, unconditional love.

Every molecule of my body was pulsating with love and light. It was the most incredible sensation. I felt more alive than ever before. It felt like I was experiencing the true reality, whereas my old world was just an illusion.

At that point I felt certain that I was dead but didn't feel any fear or regret. I thought about my family. As I was receiving all this healing, they would be down in the hospital, feeling desperately sad. But I didn't feel any guilt because I knew they were going to experience this amazing feeling of peace one day too.

I wondered if I'd be able to see my family now and had an idea that the old world might be somewhere down below. I looked down over my shoulder, over the edge of the slab, thinking I might see the hospital. But instead I saw a vast waterfall of stars cascading down, brightly sparkling. I kept looking down and saw galaxy after galaxy, stretching into infinity. I realized that I wasn't in a room but was lying among the stars. I looked back at the brilliant tunnel of light and understood that all the love I could feel — the love in the hands of the beings and in the colors and the darkness and the waterfall of stars — was coming from the incandescent light.

At that point I lay my head back and laughed because I felt so joyous. Then suddenly I was back in the hospital, with an overdrive of noise and light and people and frantic voices. I was being rushed into the operating room.

David's life was saved, and he underwent an eight-hour operation to save his arm. His consultant was amazed at his rate of recovery, which David felt was due to the support of the beings he had encountered, who were still charging him with love and energy.

Like the accident itself, David's NDE probably lasted only a few seconds in normal time but changed him in a powerful and permanent way. The feeling of new energy and love remained inside him, and he felt as though he were reborn, living a much richer and more fulfilling life. He experienced a surge of creativity and began to depict the visions of his NDE in a series of paintings. He also started to compose music. He had played guitar in pop and punk bands before, but now he began to write symphonic classical pieces as another way of conveying the incredible sense of peace and calmness he had experienced.

These changes have remained for more than fourteen years. Summarizing the effect of the experience, David told me:

I feel like I'm living in many different dimensions rather than just one. I'm much more sensitive and can pick up on the energy of places and people. It has made my life so much more interesting. I'm involved in so many different things and channeling so many different ideas. I have a sense of optimism and trust, a sense that everything happens for a reason and that things tend to work themselves out in the end, as part of a greater order.

I have a lot more appreciation for nature, and the world seems a beautiful place. I love watching animals and insects, watching the seasons change. Before the experience, I was so immersed in myself that all those things just didn't exist for me. They were just there.

It's changed my relationships too. I'm a lot more understanding rather than feeling disappointed in people. I have a much broader take on how people work. That helps me to be more supportive to those around me.

The people around me know that I've changed massively too. When I told my parents about the experience, my mother said, "We know that something's happened to you. Since the accident you're just glowing. You have this aura that is gently giving out to everyone around you."

When I asked David if he thought the experience could have been just an elaborate hallucination, he was adamant that it wasn't:

The whole thing was as real as you and I sitting here now. We're all aware of dreams, and we know that they're not real, but my experience was completely different. It was much more real than our normal experience, not less real. I felt my whole physical being was there. And I know that it wouldn't be so important to me if it had been a dream. Ever since then, my life has been all about the experience. I've started to paint and to compose classical music in order to describe it. I've never had the slightest doubt that it was real.

David's last point is a very important one. Hallucinations are never life changing. Dreams can sometimes be vivid and meaningful, but if they have any effect on us, it usually fades away quickly.

They rarely, if ever, permanently change our personality and our perspective on life. Hallucinations or dreams don't bring about a shift in our values, our perception, and our lifestyle. They don't bring about a permanent shift in which the old ego dissolves away and a latent higher spiritual self emerges in its place. (At the same time, it is possible for spiritual awakening to occur while a person is asleep and to manifest itself in remarkable dreams. We will look at two cases of this in the next chapter.) NDEs change people radically and permanently, which would be impossible if they were just hallucinations.

"The Light inside Me Has Grown" – Zak's Story

The second story I will share is fascinating because it includes both an NDE (in fact, two NDEs) and an intense mortality encounter through cancer. Zak experienced transformation from both these sources, and so his spiritual awakening was especially intense.

Zak's story is also interesting because, unlike most of the people in this book, he was interested in spirituality before his transformation. He had been a spiritual seeker for a number of years and a longtime practitioner of meditation. But, as with Ananta's prison experience described in chapter 3, his experience transformed him from a seeker into a finder.

Zak had a difficult upbringing. His father was Pakistani, while his mother was a white British woman who abandoned Zak and his sister when he was a young child. His father brought him and his sister up as strict Muslims. He never saw his mother again.

At about the age of three, Zak had meningitis and almost died. In fact, he apparently did die, at least for a short time. He doesn't recall the details of his illness, but his father told him years later that the doctor told him he was unlikely to survive. The imam was called to give him his last rites. However, Zak remembers the details of his NDE quite vividly:

I was in a tunnel and felt two presences, one on each side of my shoulders. I remember feeling floaty and disoriented and not knowing where I was. There was a pin of light in the distance, a bright light that caught my attention.

I float toward it and it gets bigger as it gets closer and closer. There appears to be some form of communication between the two presences and me, but I can't discern what it is or what form it takes. But I feel like they're guiding me to the bright light.

As I enter the bright light, I feel like I'm entering into unimaginable unconditional love. I feel completely free, with no sense of lack. I'm bathing in the light. There's no sense of outer or inner, but I can still discern the boundaries of me, even though I'm not a body at this point.

All I want to do is stay in the light. There's no urge to do anything. The light is both inside and outside me. And at the same time the light has its own consciousness that is manifesting internally and externally. I remain in the light for about fifteen minutes, and then I sense that there are other beings around, sharing the light with me. I feel a twinge of jealousy that they are experiencing the light too. I feel like it should just be mine.

As soon as I experience that, I feel that I cannot stay here. I feel a sadness and reluctance to ever leave, but I sense that I have unfinished business elsewhere that I can't ignore. I begin to realize that there are things I have to do. I don't want to leave the light. I'm trying to ignore the feeling. But it won't let me. I feel that there is no choice. I have to go back.

There was so much reluctance, but eventually I found myself being pulled into the tunnel against my will. And that's as far as I remember.

Zak didn't tell his parents or anyone else about the experience. He sensed intuitively that it didn't happen to other people and began to withdraw, perceiving himself as different. The experience began to recede into an unconscious memory. He even forgot that he had had meningitis and come close to death. In fact, he didn't recall this NDE at all until years later, when he read a book about

NDEs, and then spoke to his father and read his medical records. However, as Zak says, "it was always there in the background. It was a fundamental change. Intuitively, deep inside myself, I knew there was more. But in having that certainty, I knew that I couldn't talk about it. There was no external validation."

As he grew up, Zak felt unhappy and alienated. He was angry with life and felt different because he knew there was more to life than everyday reality. Being mixed race and lacking a sense of belonging added to this feeling of alienation. After a period of trying to escape from his frustration by partying, he decided to study psychology and philosophy at university. "I was seeking answers. I felt betrayed, so I wanted to find truth."

Shortly after starting at the university, at a time when he was so depressed that he was seriously contemplating suicide, Zak had a powerful awakening experience:

> I was coming up to the main university building. I turned a corner and looked toward a tree that caught my attention. It was luminous. It literally had an outer sheath of unimaginable translucent light. It took my breath away. I felt oneness with the light, and the tree just shone in brilliance and breathtaking beauty. Nothing existed for about thirty seconds. However, to me it felt like a timeless series of moments.
>
> The tree was situated on a very busy roundabout with lots of people milling around and lots of cars passing by, but they all dissolved. After about thirty seconds the mundanity of life came back. But that experience changed everything. There was a tingling feeling all over my skin. It woke me up to the reality of what poets like Blake were writing about. It really shook my way of looking at the world. It was a catalyst that began to shift me from one level of consciousness to another.

Zak had the opportunity to go to America to study for the second year of his studies. There he became friendly with a spiritual seeker who introduced him to Buddhism and Sufism. After voraciously reading books on spirituality, he started to meditate and eventually became a vegetarian. From this point on, spirituality was the main theme of his life. When he returned to England, his family felt that he had become a different person and were puzzled.

After graduating, Zak moved to a different part of the UK with his wife. (Afraid that he wouldn't return home, his father and stepmother had quickly arranged for him to be married before he went to the States.) He started to work as a psychology lecturer at a college, at the same time spending a lot of time meditating and following his spiritual interests. (It was around this time that Zak found the book about NDEs at his local library and recalled his own experience.)

In 2009 — by which time he had amicably divorced his wife — Zak began to feel ill. He had severe bruising on his legs, from his knees down to his ankles. His whole body seemed to be breaking down, with an enlarged spleen, heart palpitations, profuse sweating, breathlessness, and sharp pain. He was eventually admitted into the hospital and told that he had acute myeloid leukemia.

While being treated for his illness, Zak had another NDE — or as he prefers to call it, a "conscious death experience." According to a friend who was visiting at the time, the medical emergency that triggered the experience lasted two to three minutes, but for Zak, the period seemed to last several hours. It included a series of incredible experiences that changed his life:

I was sitting in bed, in a very buoyant mood, talking to my friend. Without warning, from the center of the back of my skull, I felt the most tsunami-like magnetic force pull on me inwardly. It was so giant in its strength that I knew it was futile to resist it. At the same time my eyes rolled 180 degrees back into their sockets. My breath shortened so much that I involuntarily gasped for air.

I hear my friend panicking, shouting my name. As I hear her run out of the room, my consciousness is drawn inward. I try to orientate myself, to establish where I could possibly be. I feel like I'm lying on a very soft cloud in darkness. I can see shards of silver light in the darkness. I feel a sense of total peace, a peace beyond understanding that completely embraces me. I feel totally comfortable. I begin to sink through the cloud. As I'm sinking, I start to wonder: What happens when I come out on the other side? Will I fall?

As I come through the cloud, I realize I'm on top of another cloud. I can hear my friend in the distance, shouting down the corridor, "Nurse! Nurse!" But I'm not disturbed at all. I'm in total peace. I realize that the cancer pain is no longer present. I'm floating through the darkness, passing through clouds, sinking through cloud after cloud, in a beautiful, buoyant way. It's an incredible feeling.

The hospital is no longer in my awareness. I can't hear my friend anymore. Then I notice that my body is somehow beginning to dissolve. I sense my toes are dissolving, like sand passing through an egg timer. I feel so peaceful that I'm not worried. I'm just curious, wondering what's happening. The dissolving process continues up to my knees. I feel immensely free and realize that I have no physical form. I feel expansive and nebulous, with no pain and no restriction.

It occurs to me to try to locate myself, to find out where I am. When you've been meditating for years you get used to exploring your inner space. But I can't locate myself. So I go into my mind, searching for the last thing I can remember. I feel my attention moving from my heart to my mind, to the spaces where concepts exist. But the concept of hospital isn't there. There's nothing there. I should be terrified, but I'm not.

The concept of family comes into awareness. Ah, yes, family, but who is my family? I can't recall. Concepts are dissolving. I lock onto the concept of gender but can't identify what my gender is. Similarly, the concepts of race and religion are present, but I can't say what race or religion I am. I try to go back to family, but the concept has dissolved. All concepts have dissolved. And yet I still exist and I am in total peace.

As I'm sinking and enjoying the sense of freedom and peace,

I hear the words "Zak! Be careful!" in a very sharp tone that jolts me. Where am I? What do I need to be careful of? Suddenly, I realize that there is a line I'm about to cross — not a line in a physical sense but some sort of demarcation. I try to negotiate. I want to stay in the peace. I don't want to go anywhere just yet. I'm free of the pain of cancer.

Time skips, and then there is another "Zak!" that is more urgent and powerful. My being attunes to where I am, and I realize that I'm a hair's breadth away from crossing the line. I realize that if I cross this line I won't be able to come back.

I don't react. I enter into the peace again. I become aware that I've crossed the line and simultaneously realize that the density around me has changed. The vibration of my environment is very fine, very subtle. I'm in a different space. There is no cognition, just pure knowingness.

I sense that the laws of this environment are far more responsive. There's a little bit of confusion, and as I'm trying to figure out what's going on, I feel a wave of energy coming from what seems to be my left. As the wave passes through me, I feel rage, anger, hostility, and fury. I turn to the left, and see, from what seems like thousands of miles away, a red ribbon-like energy structure. I feel a slight trepidation.

As I'm contemplating this, I feel another wave of energy from my right. As this wave passes through me, I feel forgiveness, expansion, welcoming, and receptivity. The color is mauve, purple, lilac. It's from another energy center, which seems like it's a thousand miles away. Without any volition, I feel the hub of my energy center and the hub of this energy center moving toward each other. I feel that I'm being pulled by the center of my heart, my own energy hub.

I don't have any memories of what happened right after that. The next memory I have is of translucent, luminous light. This light has a different quality from the light I experienced in meditation and in my first NDE. It's incredibly pure. Immediately I know that this level of purity doesn't exist in the normal world. It's completely untainted, so pure, so full of loving-kindness that my whole being is weeping with gratitude. My whole body is imbued with translucent light. It's humbling beyond measure. I feel an incredible tenderness. The best metaphor is the way a newborn baby is held by its mother, its head in the palm of her hand, in the softest, most gentle way. It's like that but multiplied thousands of times. I'm touched by the light. Even now, eleven years later, I feel such immense gratitude for the experience.

Then I feel movement upward. It feels like I'm moving up through a shaft, at a high speed, something like 70 or 80 miles an hour. The darkness becomes lighter and lighter, like a diver rising back up to the surface of a lake, as the light beams penetrate the darkness of the sea. I sense myself being raised horizontally and I feel myself fusing back into body. Simultaneously, at the exact same time, my eyes roll back and open and I feel like I'm locking back into my body. I know that I'm okay and attempt to take my oxygen mask off, with doctors and nursing rushing around, telling me to leave it on.

It took about four hours for my mind to come back and another three weeks to grasp the experience. Why was I pushed back? I wanted to stay there, but I had to come back. I was angry that I'd had to come back.

After several months of treatment — including more than fifty blood transfusions — Zak's cancer went into remission. However, he was left with a variety of health problems. He experienced years of chronic fatigue, which led to him breaking his back in a fall. He went through a period of depression and had to cope with bone pain on a daily basis. The illness has left him partially blind in one eye, with a sensitive stomach and overall frailty.

Despite these ongoing health issues, Zak feels immensely grateful for the gifts he received during his NDE and his illness. He told me that if he ever writes a book, he will call it *The Gifts of Cancer*. His illness and his encounters with death have shifted him out of spiritual seeking and into "a state of spiritual abiding," as he calls it.

Summarizing the changes he has undergone, Zak told me:

It's fundamentally transformed me. In this world we chase status, possessions, and apparent truths, but none of these things matter in the slightest if they aren't grounded in the truth of your own heart. It seems to me after my experience that all spiritual practice is ultimately about the transformation of the heart. If I die tomorrow, the only thing that will endure or truly matter is what's in my heart.

An expansion has occurred. I feel like the light inside me has grown. Sometimes I get a headache and sometimes I get angry, but that's all right. The light is always there. It comes through. The light is always with me.

The whole universe derives its very existence from this light. Without this light nothing is able to exist. One truth I have become aware of is that there is no inherent substance to reality. Only the light has any "real reality." I've become aware of further truths, and I suspect that there are others waiting. As such, it has become a deepening and broadening. And this deepening and broadening have no end.

As I was preparing this book for publication, Zak contacted me to tell me that — after nine years in remission — his cancer has returned. As I write this, he has just completed his first round of chemotherapy and is having regular blood transfusions. He feels tired and sick, and has periods of pain, but remains in a state of calm acceptance. He told me, "I trust in the universe. I'm at peace with whatever happens."

The Light

As well as being amazing stories of spiritual awakening — and inspiring stories of the indomitability of the human spirit in the face of intense suffering — David's and Zak's stories raise some interesting questions about the nature of reality. The two most striking aspects of their experiences are the translucent light they perceived and their intense sense of joy and peace. They both described the light as brighter and purer than any light on earth, although it didn't hurt them or blind their eyes. It was both external and internal, pervading all space and immersing their being. As it immersed them, both David and Zak felt overwhelmed with love and bliss. As David remarked, "it was the light of pure, unconditional love." Both David and Zak also described the light as a fundamental quality. David described it as "the source of all creation," while Zak stated that "the whole universe derives its very existence from this light."

In fact, most people who have NDEs report seeing a translucent light and feeling intense joy. It's beyond the scope of this book to look into these issues in detail, but I firmly believe that, as both David and Zak suggest, this translucent light *is* a fundamental quality of the universe. In my book *Spiritual Science*, I describe the philosophy of "panspiritism," which suggests that there is a fundamental spiritual force at the heart of reality, which pervades all space and all material things, including living beings. This spiritual force — or "fundamental consciousness," as I sometimes call it — gives rise to the material world. All physical forms emerge from it, like plants emerging from the soil. And this fundamental consciousness or spirit has a quality of translucent light. Like a star, it radiates translucent light.

In Indian philosophy, this fundamental consciousness is referred to as *brahman*, the radiant spiritual force that pervades the world and constitutes (as *atman*) the inner spirit of human beings. As the Bhagavad-Gita says of *brahman*, "If the light of a thousand suns suddenly arose in the sky, that splendour might be compared to the radiance of the Supreme Spirit."[11] Similarly, the thirteenth-century Christian mystic Meister Eckhart believed that the ultimate reality was not God but "the Godhead," whose essence is light. God is an emanation of the Godhead. Meister Eckhart also believed that the essence of the human soul was light, in the same way that *atman* is of the same nature as *brahman*. So according to Meister Eckhart, when we become one with God, there is a merging of light with light.

In our normal state of awareness, we are unable to sense this fundamental consciousness, with its qualities of light, love, and bliss. Our restricted awareness may even deceive us into seeing the world as a cold, empty, and even hostile place. But in NDEs (and in awakening experiences) our awareness slips free of the filtering structures of the mind. It feels as if a veil has been lifted, allowing us to glimpse the fundamental reality of the universe. This reality is so overwhelmingly real and powerful and meaningful that we undergo permanent transformation.

Another fascinating aspect of both David's and Zak's reports is the beings or presences they encountered. These were a very significant aspect of David's experience — he encountered a being of light and two other, darker-skinned beings who spread their hands over his body and healed him. Zak didn't encounter any beings or presences in his second NDE, but in his first, when he was about three years old, he was aware of two presences who guided him to a bright light. He was also aware of presences who were sharing the light with him. (Interestingly, he remembers feeling jealous of them, wishing the light could be his alone, which perhaps reflects the narcissism of early childhood.)

Like the light and a sense of love and bliss, such beings or presences are often a feature of near-death experiences. If we accept that NDEs are not hallucinations, then we have to be open to the possibility that these beings are real entities, whose presence we can detect only when our awareness becomes much more intense and expansive than normal.

The Five Angels

It is tempting to wonder whether these beings of light are the origin of the concept of angels. In particular, David's description of a luminous white being seems reminiscent of an angel. In connection with this, I would like to end this chapter with one final story. This is a case in which beings of light were seen by a person who witnessed a death rather than a person who died for a short time. Strictly speaking, it is a case of transformation through bereavement. But since it features the same type of beings or presences that David and Zak encountered, it seems appropriate to include it here.

In 2016 a fifteen-year-old girl named Natasha Ednan-Laperouse died from an allergic reaction after eating a sandwich. Her father, Nadim, was with her at the moment she died. Paramedics tried to restart her heart, and Natasha recovered consciousness for a few seconds. But then her heartbeat faded again. At that point, Nadim looked up and saw five luminous figures — who he immediately thought of as angels — around his daughter's body: "These five angels just appeared, and this yellow light, strong, soft yellow light, rather like candlelight but really intense." He described the figures as "about twenty centimeters tall, not chubby like children in a Renaissance painting and with feathery wings like the Vatican, but actually like human beings, all looking at me, moving around Natasha." He instinctively felt that they had come to take his daughter away, which meant that she was about to die. He waved them away, shouting, "This is not her time!" Then the beings disappeared. And at precisely that moment, Natasha died.

Nadim was an atheist, so his vision of angels was especially startling. He was also certain that the vision wasn't a hallucination. As he put it, "I am the least likely person to have an hallucination. I am not prone to such things ever. I've always been calm and stalwart in moments of adversity and stress. What have I to gain by making this up?"

Nadim had another powerful experience a few months after his daughter's death. He started to campaign for better labeling on food products to help other people with allergies. One day he learned that the British prime minister, Theresa May, had taken up the cause. He felt overwhelmed with gratitude and started to cry. As he described it, "Suddenly the whole room lit up like someone had put the light on but not the normal light. It was a soft yellow light again that I remember from seeing the angels. I was so taken aback I remember going, 'Oh my gosh! What's that?' And as I did that, the light went."[12]

For Nadim these experiences — together, no doubt, with the trauma of his bereavement — were transformational. He recognized that previously he had been an arrogant and self-centered person, focused on success and profit. Now he became much more humble, open, and loving. As is sometimes the case with shifters who are unfamiliar with any forms of spirituality except traditional religion, Nadim interpreted his experience in Christian terms. Convinced that he had seen angels around his daughter's body, and that the light he had seen was a communication with God, he decided to convert to Christianity and is now a regular churchgoer.

The Process of Dying

We can't say anything certain about death. We will never find out for sure whether the light is a fundamental reality of the universe or whether beings of light (or angels) really exist until we actually die ourselves.

At some point — when we are seriously ill or old and infirm, or if we have an accident or sudden injury — we are all going to have an intense mortality encounter. And interestingly, there is evidence to suggest that this encounter will be transformational for most of us. In 2015 the Swiss psychotherapist Monika Renz led a team of researchers who investigated the experiences of 680 dying patients in hospices. The researchers found that most patients went through a transition into a different state of consciousness, moving beyond anxiety and pain and into acceptance and peace.

Based on her findings, Renz has identified three stages of the dying process: pretransition, transition, and post-transition. In the pretransition phase, there is fear and resistance. But as patients move through transition, the structures and attachments of the ego fade away, and there is a growing sense of trust and well-being. This intensifies through the post-transition phase, where there is a state of liberation from the ego, with tranquility and bliss. As Renz describes it, "Patients feel free and at the same time somehow connected, a connectedness with the universe, with a transcendental sphere."[13]

These findings are supported by the relatives and caregivers of dying people. It is surprisingly common for people to die peacefully and serenely, in a state of acceptance. Many dying people appear to see — and speak to — deceased relatives, as if the relatives are greeting them. It is almost as if, on the verge of death, people are already at home in another world. They appear to be experiencing something of the intense feelings of love, bliss, and freedom described by David and Zak above.

Renz found that more than half of the dying patients proceeded to the post-transition phase and so experienced a spiritual opening. She believes that the true figure may have been higher but that a number of other patients were "either unable, or too shy, or too tired to contribute" to her study.[14]

These findings suggest that most of us will experience spiritual awakening when we come to face death. Even if we don't return from an NDE or IME earlier in our lives, the enormous spiritual potential of death may well transform us eventually, in the final days, hours, or minutes of our lives.

6

ON THE BRINK OF SUICIDE

Transformation through Depression and Stress

The term *depression* is very apt, in that the condition feels like psychological pressure bearing down on us. It burdens us with a sense of hopelessness and sadness, sapping our energy and motivation. Often it's related to an inner dialogue of negative thoughts, convincing us that we are useless, that we don't deserve to be loved, that we are bound to fail at everything we do, and so on. There seems to be an observer in our heads, commentating as we act and speak, criticizing our behavior, and reacting negatively to our circumstances and prospects.

The pressure of depression may become so intense that we feel an impulse to kill ourselves in order to free ourselves from it. At the same time, such suicidal impulses are often an expression of self-hatred. We hate ourselves so much that we feel a strong desire to injure and destroy ourselves.

Some of the shifters we've heard from so far suffered from depression owing to specific events and situations. For example, in chapter 4, Suzy and Renee were deeply depressed due to their bereavements. But as we all know, depression can also arise in a subtler way, with sources that are difficult to pinpoint. Some psychiatrists have a simplistic belief that depression is caused by a chemical im-balance in the brain. It is supposedly associated with a low level of a neurotransmitter called serotonin, and depressed people are routinely prescribed medication that increases their serotonin lev-els. However, as I pointed out in my book *Spiritual Science*, very little evidence backs up this assumption. Depression is much more strongly related to environmental and existential factors than neu-rological ones. The condition is related to people's life situations, their jobs and relationships, their negative thought patterns, a lack of purpose and meaning, a lack of contact with nature, a lack of physical exercise, too much stress and activity, and so on.

In some cases, depression may also be *spiritual* in origin. Spir-itual depression occurs when a person is alienated from their spir-itual nature. Many people have a certain degree of innate spiritual wakefulness, even if it's just a seed that they yearn to cultivate by fol-lowing spiritual practices or paths. However, if their culture doesn't accept or support spirituality, they may not understand or accept their own spiritual nature. Their spiritual impulses and experiences may create confusion, resistance, and even self-hatred. In other cases, people may actually undergo spiritual awakening at a young age but be unable to process or understand the experience.

Such people may have to repress their spirituality, which causes a huge amount of frustration. They may also feel a strong sense of inauthenticity and self-hatred, because they feel obliged to live an incongruous lifestyle, following the conventions of their culture in-stead of their own spiritual impulses. (As I described in *The Leap*, I went through periods of spiritual depression myself, during which I often thought about committing suicide. I finally emerged from this depression fully at around the age of twenty-nine.)

In this chapter, we're going to look at cases of TTT triggered by long periods of intense depression. The first two cases were very clearly linked to spiritual depression, involving early spiritual awak-enings that were repressed. The third case is slightly different, in that the obvious cause of the transformation was a long period of intense stress, along with childhood trauma that wasn't acknowledged or dealt with.

"I Feel Like the Universe Is Holding Me" – Donna's Story

Donna Thomas is an academically gifted woman in her forties, from the north of England. She has a PhD in psychology and works as a researcher at a university. I met Donna for the first time when she gave a presentation at a Transpersonal Psychology conference in the UK in 2018. I had the strange sensation that I had known her for a long time. From the start, speaking to her was like talking to an old friend with whom I felt at ease. Her conference presentation had a powerful impact, because it was clear that she had undergone a transformation that had endowed her with deep spiritual insight.

Donna had suffered from a deep depression. A major source of this depression was her traumatic childhood, caused by her mother's alcoholism. She had a good relationship with her father, but he traveled for work most of the time, and at home she suffered emotional abuse and neglect. (Her parents divorced when she was ten, and she went to live with her father.) Donna's first spiritual experience occurred at the age of five, when she was run over by a motorcycle. The bike landed on top of her, then the biker sped off. While she was lying on the pavement, she felt as if she were high up in the air, looking all around. She could see all the streets in the neighborhood, as if from above. As Donna told me, "It was my first taste of an awareness that things are not quite as they seem."

This was followed by a near-death experience when Donna was fifteen. Late one night, a friend offered her a lift home but drove much too fast in torrential rain. He lost control of the car, which flipped over four times and crashed into a wall. The car was on fire, upside down, and they were trapped in it:

I remember the terror and the pain. The thought came up that I was going to die, and it was terrifying. Then all of a sudden there was just the most beautiful feeling. It was difficult to express, but I was in the most serene state ever. I wasn't in the car. I wasn't anywhere. I didn't feel like a fifteen-year-old girl anymore. There was this all-pervading love, and everything felt expansive. I felt expansive. I had a sense that I was returning home. I was nowhere yet everywhere. Time vanished. And in that space with no name, no definitions, I saw my whole life – every single event that I had ever been involved in flashing by, every event, one after the other. I felt so much love for everything and everyone in that scenario, for family members, friends, and enemies alike.

Then as quick as anything I was back in the burning car, upside down, with the feeling of terror, tangled up in the bent metal and leather that was once the back seat of my friend's car. I was sure I was going to die. But then a truck driver smashed the window and pulled us out.

Fortunately, I didn't have any serious injuries. I had a broken nose and whiplash. I was bedbound for two weeks, and in a blissful state. I didn't know why I was so happy. It wasn't that I was happy to be alive. I was just full of bliss. The doctor thought there was something wrong with me and kept saying that I was in shock. Everyone who came in the room seemed like a beautiful being. I felt so full of love for everyone I saw.

Donna's background was completely nonreligious, and she knew nothing about NDEs or spirituality. After her initial euphoria began to fade, she felt confused. She started to have spiritual experiences but felt threatened by them. She told me, "The sky was falling down on me. I was probably merging with the sky, having expansive experiences, but I didn't understand it so it scared me. I tried to tell people about it, and about my experience in the car, but nobody understood."

Spiritual awakenings are also spiritual *openings*. They open us up to a wider and more intense vision of reality. This is an invigorating experience, but if the opening occurs suddenly and dramatically, it may also feel overwhelming. In addition, as our ego boundaries fall away, there may be a release of repressed pain and trauma within our psyche. Donna experienced an emergence of childhood trauma, along with other material she didn't understand. She was offered medication but had an intuition that she shouldn't take it.

The next four years were very difficult:

> I was in a state of confusion and depression, wondering whether I was insane. I knew there was something outside normal reality, but I didn't know what it was. I tried to function as a normal person, but I couldn't hold down a job. I really wanted to talk about what was happening to me but felt completely isolated. There were times when I couldn't go out. I found it very difficult to speak to people. I was very trapped in the mind. My experience had changed from being this incredible blissful space inside me to my being completely caught up in the mind's narrative.

In response to her confusion and depression, Donna felt the impulse to create a new self-narrative. At nineteen, she had a baby, which gave her an identity as a mother. The accident when she was fifteen had disrupted her education, and she had left school with no qualifications. Now she decided to go back to school. She studied to be a secretary and did so well that one of her teachers suggested she do a degree. She sailed through her degree so easily that one of her tutors suggested she do a master's degree, which led to a part-time PhD. She became a linguist, studying the structures and uses of language, and adopted the viewpoint that there is nothing more to reality than language.

At the same time as she was studying and bringing up her daughter, Donna was building a successful career in local government. She became a strategic manager, writing policies for her local council. She was proficient in her job, and very driven. At the same time, she was, in her own words, "becoming very cold, very uncaring, very sealed off. I was building an armor. It was a huge escape."

But eventually, when Donna was forty, the armor broke open. Several years before that, her father (whom she remained very close to) had suddenly dropped dead from a heart attack. A year later, she had met a man with narcissistic tendencies, leading to a difficult marriage. Her husband would subtly control and manipulate her until she began to lose her perspective on reality. "I was paralyzed with fear," she told me. "Everything began to unravel. I left my job and couldn't do anything. I had all these intrusive thoughts that didn't seem to belong to me. I had strong emotions, severe anxiety, and bouts of what seemed to be psychosis. It went on for about twelve months, and it got so severe that I just didn't want to live anymore."

Donna gave me a written account of the transformational experience that followed from her intense turmoil:

As my husband collected my son, I knew that I wouldn't be seeing him again. I knew that he would be far better off without me in his life. My intention was to go upstairs and first plan out a way to die. I had lots of painkillers in the cupboard, and that could be an option, said one of the several voices that were chaotically playing at once. I knew that I was going to die. As I closed the door, saying goodbye to my son, the constant shaking I had been experiencing began to reach a peak, and my body began to feel very weak. The shaking became severe and heat rushed through my body to the point where I felt suffocated. The pains in my body (particularly my legs) became so bad that I half walked, half crawled up the stairs. The heat was searing so much I had to remove my clothes, and I collapsed onto the bed. I then found myself moving through a thick black tunnel. As I moved through, aspects of trauma in the form of images, smells, sounds, and emotions merged and I felt every aspect of their content. I had a strong sense that I was about to die, and I surrendered. Fear dissolved and I fell into tunnel after tunnel. This lasted several hours through the night, including all the bodily pains and discomfort.

As the sun shone through the window, as morning arrived, a large part of who I believed myself to be had gone. I felt some peace for the first time since I was a child. My mind was still. I had no idea what had happened to me, nor did I care. What I did feel was a sense of new beginnings and reconnections to something that I could not quite understand.

Perhaps because it had been repressed for so long, Donna's awakening twenty-five years earlier reemerged with great force. It heralded a permanent transformation, a shift into a higher functioning state. From that point on, she was a different person, with an ongoing sense of lightness, expansiveness, and well-being.

However, it took her a long time to adjust to her new expansive awareness. After a sudden and dramatic transformation, it can take a long time for our organism to settle down again. Once the old structures of the psyche have dissolved away, new structures need to establish themselves, which can be a long process. This is why — as we've seen in many cases throughout this book — spiritual awakening is often not the blissful and easy transition that many seekers imagine. As with her first awakening at the age of fifteen, Donna found that the sudden breaking open of her psyche allowed a lot of unfamiliar and unsettling experiences to come through. She described the aftermath of her experience:

For about a year it was very hard because I was living in a different reality. Everything was very slow. Time didn't exist. Even when I was with my loved ones, I experienced them as a field of energy rather than as people.

A lot of things were coming up too. I had telepathic experiences and out-of-body experiences. I had hypnogogic experiences where I traveled to past lives. I experienced searing pains in my legs that put me in bed for a couple of days. Once I realized that the pain was trapped trauma from both my accidents, it moved.

At this stage, Donna still didn't know anything about spirituality, so her sense of expansive well-being was again offset by a sense of confusion. As with her NDE, she didn't have a conceptual framework to understand her transformation. Several years earlier, a friend had given her a copy of *The Power of Now* by Eckhart Tolle. After a brief look, she had thrown it on top of one of her bookshelves and forgotten about it. About six weeks after her transformation, she was walking past her bookshelf when, in her words,

> Somehow it fell off the top shelf and hit me on the head and fell on the floor. As I bent down to pick it up it was open to a page that talked about the pain body. I began to read and felt a further shift and resonance. The book was a tipping point because it was talking about what I was experiencing. It was the first time that my experience was validated. It opened me up to the world of spirituality. It was the start of a process of integration for me.

My research suggests that, no matter how much disturbance and confusion they might initially cause, sudden and dramatic awakenings almost always settle down eventually, even if it takes years. Seven years after her transformation, Donna now feels that it is well integrated. She is able to function well in the world — in fact, at a much higher level than before, now that she feels she is living authentically, with a powerful sense of connection and a strong desire to serve others:

> It's nowhere near as difficult as it was. I'm much more integrated. The space is always there. People sometimes ask me, "Do you meditate?" And I don't, because life is the meditation, when you meet it from that space. You are that space all the time, not just when you sit down to meditate.
>
> When it first happened, everything appeared on the surface of that space. Now it's more in the background, although there are still times when it's really intense. At night, when I'm lying in bed, I just drop into the space and silence. And when I wake up it's still there, and I go through the day from that space.

It's interesting because life has been quite challenging with my family and as a parent, but I can deal with the challenges. You can't ever leave the world behind. You can't just go and sit in a cave. We can't detach ourselves from the world.

Before, the world was a really scary place. It was very cold and frightening – there was a sense that I didn't belong. I felt like an alien. People frightened me. I thought everyone was selfish and out for themselves, and I wouldn't trust anybody. But now everything is absolutely sacred. People may have patterns that cause unpleasant behavior, but if you can look past that, everyone is just a sacred being.

Now I can just sit and be with the sky and the trees, feeling my feet in the grass. They didn't even exist for me before. Every moment I feel I am in deep gratitude. I used to be such a competitive and insecure person, very concerned with status and materialism and possessions. That was part of my armor. But now the armor has gone and I'm much more open and less selfish. I used to be so anxious to get somewhere, but now I feel like the universe is holding me. You don't need to know where you're going – things just happen and unfold. Just let it drop, and live with trust.

In recent years, Donna has returned to academia. She is now a researcher at Lancaster University, specializing in how children experience the world, particularly children who are in crisis or who are struggling to accept the world as it appears because of their innate spirituality or giftedness. She is also investigating spirituality from an academic perspective, through the field of transpersonal psychology.

"I Feel More Carefree Than I Ever Have in My Life" – Parker's Story

It is significant that Donna's transformation occurred when she was at the point of suicide. When a person wants to kill themselves, it's a sign that their ego has been completely broken down.

Their depression and self-hatred have cracked the shell of their ego identity. They have been stripped of everything — all hopes, all self-esteem, all attachments to success or possessions or social roles. After all, if they were attached to any of these things, they wouldn't want to let go of them and wouldn't want to kill themselves. At the same time, a suicidal intention signals a point of surrender. It's the point at which the ego gives up and stops trying. It therefore represents a point of acceptance. And as I have already suggested, TTT is often generated by an attitude of acceptance, following an experience of ego-dissolution.

This was certainly the case in the next story, which was shared with me by a Canadian man named Parker, who also reached the point of seriously contemplating suicide. Perhaps even more so than Donna's, Parker's depression was mainly spiritual in origin, due to the repression of a spiritual awakening when he was eighteen.

During his childhood, Parker was bullied and had few friends. Desperate to gain some status and popularity, at the age of fourteen he started to sell drugs to his high school friends. At first he sold pot, then moved on to psychedelics. However, he was caught selling marijuana and expelled from school. His parents threw him out of the house too, so that at the age of sixteen, he found himself living alone. This led to a period of heavy drug use, which lasted for two years:

I ended up getting heavily addicted to cocaine, as well as doing meth and other drugs. I was really screwed up for a young teenager. I couldn't see any purpose to my existence. I was very unwell, mentally and physically. I'm six foot one, and my weight went down to 120 pounds.

There was a period at the end when I was awake for close to a week, constantly doing drugs. I was expecting to die of an overdose, and I was kind of okay with that. I finally fell asleep, and when I woke up the next day, I suddenly wasn't addicted anymore. It was incredibly bizarre. I called my sister and said, "I'm done with all this. I'm not taking drugs anymore. Can you come and pick me up?" She was amazed because I hadn't seen her – or my parents – for more than a year.

It was bizarre at the time, but the feeling I had then was the same as now. I was convinced that I was God and that everyone around me was God. It occurred to me that everyone was running around worrying about this and that and missing the picture. I felt like everyone around me was crazy. But I couldn't communicate with anyone. I couldn't put it into words.

I went to see a psychiatrist, and I knew that if I told him what I was feeling I'd end up in a psychiatric ward. So I put on a veneer of normality. He couldn't understand how my addiction had just disappeared. He said there was maybe some kind of impact on my frontal lobe, which is connected with addiction or desire or craving. He said it wasn't normal for people to suddenly be free of addiction, particularly when you're doing drugs so heavily on a daily basis.

I didn't know how to interpret the experience at the time, which is why I don't think it had much of a lasting impact. I tried to meditate for a couple of years afterward and read *Way of the Peaceful Warrior* and the *Tao Te Ching*. That was the extent of my "spiritual studies" back then.

I quit drugs completely and went back to school and did very well. I forgot about that initial experience. I wrote it off as some strange but lucky turning point. I thought it was maybe just some chemical change in my mind, like the psychiatrist said. Instead of looking inward, I began to look outward for happiness in the form of "success." I went on a continual path of adding to myself, working toward this better future, looking to succeed. I got lost in the outwardness of it all.

By his early thirties, Parker seemed to have every reason to be happy. He had a successful profession and a comfortable, affluent lifestyle. He was also happily married and had a young daughter. But despite his social and material success, he felt a gnawing sense of fear and meaninglessness. Parker said, "I couldn't see any point to my own existence. I was searching for happiness outside myself with the underlying understanding that whatever I accomplished wasn't going to get me that state of being truly happy." His spiritual depression was aggravated by the stress of his job as a conflict lawyer, which was so full of tension that he sometimes had panic attacks. He felt depressed almost all the time and began to contemplate suicide: "Most days would start with me crying in the shower, wishing I didn't have to live in my own skin."

The impulse to kill himself grew stronger during a family vacation in Japan. He was supposed to be relaxing, but the free time made him feel more anxious. He told me, "The more time I had to not be distracted but to instead be alone with my own thoughts, the worse I felt and the more meaningless my life seemed." During the vacation, he regularly walked past a bridge near the house where he was staying, and each time he thought about throwing himself off:

On December 30 [2019], I stood by the bridge for perhaps three hours trying to gather the resolve to jump but couldn't work up the courage. I went back to my in-laws' house feeling completely miserable, with the idea in my mind that I would go back and try again the next day. I spent the remainder of the afternoon and evening feeling possibly the most miserable I've ever felt. I went to bed around midnight.

In my sleep I had an incredibly vivid dream in which I could fly through cities and in between planets, meet with my deceased grandparents, and all sorts of things that I've since forgotten. It had me feeling mind-blown and euphoric. I woke at 8 a.m., and a complete calm overtook not just my mind but my body as well. My lower back had been in pain for months, but the pain seemed not to bother me anymore. Everything I experienced in each moment felt perfect, whether it was the sound of birds chirping, the sight of wind blowing through the trees, or old men fishing by the river behind the home. Even when sitting down or standing up, my body felt different, as though suddenly I had become aware of all the different parts of my body. It was as if my soul had been occupying this body for my entire life but I never gave a second thought to what it felt like until now, or I just wasn't paying attention to the feeling of living in my body.

The most profound aspect was that the thoughts that used to begin the moment I woke up in the morning and subside only when I fell asleep had now suddenly ceased to arise in my mind at all. I don't actually have any memory of thoughts arising for most of the day on December 31. There was a degree of euphoria in every experience that I can't easily describe, but it was undoubtedly the best morning of my entire life. I was mostly speechless the entire day.

It is remarkable that Parker's transformation occurred while he was asleep. It seems to have manifested itself in his lucid dream. He didn't consciously experience the moment of transformation itself — since it happened while he was unconscious — but became aware of it when he woke up. He described the change as "akin to flipping a drastic switch." It is clear that, from the moment of waking up that morning, he was a different person.

Parker originally wrote to me because he was seeking to understand his transformation. He had started to read books on spirituality and came across my writings. At the time I was in contact with him, it was only six months since his shift, but his previous state of being already seemed like a distant memory, a remote state that it would be impossible to return to:

I don't feel even the slightest degree of anxiety, sadness, depression, frustration, or concern about anything. It's as though my entire identity and ego just dissolved overnight, to the point where I feel more carefree than I ever have in my life, even compared to being a young child.

Although the euphoric feeling isn't permanent, the raw experience is permanently accessible. I have to turn on my identity or ego for work and in order to interact with the people in my life, but I can simply turn it off or ignore it when I don't need to use my mind. While I still have thoughts, I'm in no way troubled by them. I am not my thoughts and not necessarily even the thinker of my own thoughts, but instead some sort of witness or observer of those thoughts. I've spent my entire life creating an identity based on the thoughts that come to me, but that identity has now suddenly and spontaneously revealed itself to be a complete fiction.

I came to the conclusion that the true me is simply the underlying awareness, the "experiencer" of all the things that I perceive, including thoughts and the process of thinking itself. It now became obvious that the true "me" has spent the majority of its adult life "watching" Parker struggle with this existential depression. It's as if my entire identity just vanished and the realization came to me that my core, the true "me" is just awareness itself.

It seems now as though the concept of time exists only in my conceptual mind. Time cannot exist in my direct experience of life itself — everything I perceive, everything I do, can only happen in the current moment in which it happens. This idea of this current moment, the right now, is rather difficult to articulate, but it's fundamental to my current experience of no stress, worry, anxiety, sadness, or depression — it's impossible to feel any of those experiences without slipping away from the present moment through thought.

All my old stress, anxiety, and worry stemmed from my thinking about future events. I could spend days in a row ruminating about all the bad things that might happen on a particular file, in an upcoming court appearance, or in the idea of loved ones like my parents growing ill and eventually dying. That's the biggest shift. All my anxiety, stress, and worry was based on this wandering mind. I don't do that at all anymore.

A lot of small things have changed too. I used to hate housework and chores — now I really enjoy them. I love going for walks, looking at different plants. My daughter plucks little things and you can see the two of us standing by the side of the road, staring at tiny flowers, watching the wind blow through trees, the leaves falling, and the animals. Even just watching cars drive by or people walking by is fascinating to me. The concept of boredom is completely gone. Loneliness too. It was always the worst time, when I was alone, when I would start ruminating and remind myself of how miserable I was. I didn't enjoy being alone because I would be stuck with this jerk in my head telling me that everything is wrong. But now I love it.

Overall, my life has completely changed since that dream, and yet very little externally has really changed at all. I'm in a sort of never-ending state of amazement by the mystery of life. The beautiful mystery of reality and appreciation of "my" mortality is ever-present and colors every interaction I have and every thought that comes to mind.

Parker's transformation has been very smooth. His experience is quite unusual, in that he hasn't undergone any of the disorientation and disturbance that often occur after a sudden and dramatic awakening. Although he has begun to read spiritual books in an effort to understand what happened to him, he seems to be doing so largely out of curiosity. There is no urgency to make sense of his shift to alleviate his confusion and frustration. Parker mentions that he is able to turn his work identity off and on, and to tune in and out of the "raw experience" of his wakefulness. This ability is a very important part of the process of integrating an awakened state, but it normally takes people quite a long time to learn it.

Perhaps the key to Parker's smooth transition is that his spiritual awakening actually occurred when he was eighteen, but he repressed it because he couldn't understand it. So his later experience wasn't so much a sudden and dramatic new awakening as a reemergence of a state that had already formed inside him but that had been blocked or obscured. (Admittedly, this explanation doesn't fit Donna's story. She also had an earlier spiritual awakening that she repressed and yet still underwent a very difficult transformation.)

In some ways, Parker's story is reminiscent of Eckhart Tolle's spiritual awakening, which was also very smooth and easy. As readers of *The Power of Now* know, after years of intensifying anxiety and depression, Tolle underwent a transformational experience in the middle of the night (although not while he was asleep). The next morning, he felt reborn. Although it took him a few years to understand exactly what had happened, Tolle also experienced very little disturbance or confusion — only an ongoing state of bliss and ease. Perhaps the only issue Tolle experienced was some difficulty with being active. (Famously, he spent months doing little aside from sitting on a park bench.) But Parker doesn't seem to have any difficulty in this area. He has been able to continue his work as a lawyer and even feels that he has become better at it, since he is much calmer and less prone to conflict.

Parker's description of his new state of being is also very similar to Tolle's teachings, emphasizing presence, freedom from the thinking mind, and freedom from psychological time. Skeptics might suggest that Parker is simply restating Tolle's teachings after reading his books. However, Parker had never heard of Tolle until I mentioned his name. Even now, Parker only has a passing familiarity with Tolle's work, after watching a few videos. It is clear that Parker's descriptions of his state of being show a degree of clarity and awareness that could only arise from direct experience.

"Everything Is Much More Vibrant and Real" – Simon's Story

TTT can be related to intense stress as well as intense depression. Whereas depression is an inner psychological pressure that burdens us, stress is an *external* pressure. It's a feeling of being overwhelmed by the world and unable to cope with the demands of our lives. It arises when we are bombarded with too much information and too many responsibilities and duties. We feel overstretched and overexposed, and if we're unable to rest and recharge ourselves, the discord inside us builds up to a breaking point. In this way, the outer pressure of stress can break down our ego in the same way as the inner pressure of depression.

As with depression, stress-induced awakening has figured in some of the cases we've looked at so far. For example, Ananta's awakening (in chapter 3) was partly triggered by the stress and anxiety of her imprisonment, and the exhaustion of her work, as well as a dismantling of her identity. David's gradual awakening, discussed in chapter 1, was largely triggered by the stress and anxiety of his life as a soldier, along with his encounters with death.

But of course, as we all know, ordinary life in itself can be intensely stressful, outside the context of unusual circumstances such as imprisonment and combat. The everyday challenges of work, family life, relationships, and illness may sometimes be enough to lead us to a breakdown — and also to a "shift up." I described several cases of stress-related awakenings in *The Leap* — for example, a woman who had an awakening as a new mother after a long period without sleep and a man who had an awakening at a time when he was experiencing intense stress due to work problems and his wife's serious illness.

Stress-induced awakenings are especially explosive. They are often reminiscent of what Hindu spirituality refers to as "kundalini awakening," when a powerful energy rises up inside us, from the lowest chakra at the base of the spine. According to Hindu and Tantric texts, when this energy rises up suddenly, in an uncontrolled way, it can be extremely disruptive and even dangerous.

In August 2018 a forty-six-year-old Englishman we will call Simon experienced this type of awakening. He was on vacation with his family in France, following a long period of stress due to problems at work and what he described as an "incredibly stressful relationship" with his wife. In May his stepfather had died, which added to the stress.

At the same time, Simon told me that his turmoil had some deeper roots. He had a traumatic childhood, during which he had watched a sibling die in an accident. As he told me, "I was very much someone who dealt with trauma and problems myself without asking for help." This created inner psychological pressure, in addition to the external pressure of stress. Recently, however, he had sought help from a therapist, who was treating him for stress-related depression.

Simon thought of himself as a scientist and logical thinker. He was an architect and IT expert, with no knowledge of — or interest in — spiritual issues. Like Parker, he only started reading about spirituality after his transformation in an effort to understand what had happened to him. As he told me, "It wasn't something I was working toward or expecting. It was completely spontaneous."

Remarkably, Simon's transformation, like Parker's, apparently occurred when he was asleep one day during his vacation:

I lay down for about ten minutes on my own and dozed off. I woke up and everything was different. It was like taking my contact lenses out. I lay there and looked up at the trees, and I could see a silver aura around all the leaves. I could hear insects tens of meters away. Everything became more vibrant. And I just felt an incredible sensation.

It was such an alien experience – I wasn't spiritual at all. It was completely overwhelming. It was just suddenly feeling that I was part of something. It was almost like being reborn but with the knowledge of an adult. An absolute weight came off me. Physiologically, a fifteen-year-old issue related to a digestive problem I picked up in Southeast Asia resolved that day.

In hindsight, I think it was a kundalini awakening. I was having massive rushes of energy. There was a tingling that started near the coccyx and rose up my spine and into my fingertips and up to my brain.

That was the start of it. From that point on, I had a different identity. I lost any sense of fear and guilt. Even my phobias of spiders and heights disappeared. The change was incredible. Two of my children at the time said, "Daddy – you've changed. Something's happened." I used to shout and be bad-tempered, but now I was caring and loving.

The term *spiritual opening* was coined by the transpersonal psychologists Stan and Christina Grof as an alternative to *spiritual awakening*. I think the term is very useful, since it emphasizes a sudden dissolving away of mental barriers and filters, bringing a much more expansive and intense awareness and a heightened sensitivity. You could compare it to a person who walks out of a small, dark house and suddenly finds themselves in a vast, open natural landscape, full of color and beauty and space. As we saw earlier in this chapter with Donna, the term *spiritual opening* also accounts for some of the disruptive and problematic aspects of awakening, including the emergence of repressed trauma.

Simon's experience also fits the concept of spiritual opening very closely. As with Donna, the sudden opening of his awareness has had both positive and negative aspects:

Nature is much more important to me. Colors are brighter, and I see so much more detail. Sometimes it's almost overwhelming. Everything is much more vibrant and real. During the first two months after it happened, I had to be outside all the time. I couldn't stand being inside a building.

I found myself suddenly "discovering" music, art, sculpture, color, nature, and connectivity, hearing and seeing things I never acknowledged before. I've become much more engaged with other people too. I started to really listen to them and get where they are coming from. There is a level of empathy and understanding that I didn't have before. I used to be closed off. I can go into a meeting with someone, and within seconds I can see them as a child and understand their approach and attitude. I used to meet people and think, "Don't ask me how I am, just tell me what you want." But now I really connect with people and sense what makes them feel valued.

It has been pretty bumpy though, I admit. I started going through a download phase. I was receiving images of sacred geometry and all sorts of things. I contacted my therapist and said, "All this stuff is coming to me and I can't stop it." I expected him to tell me I'd had a breakdown, but fortunately he didn't. He encouraged me to think of it as a positive experience.

At the time I spoke to Simon, it had been two years since his shift. He appeared to be adjusting to his new state, with the disturbance and disorientation beginning to fade. The rushing, rising energy he used to regularly feel had settled down. Like Parker, he has been able to continue working and feels that he has actually become better at his job due to his increased empathy and understanding of his clients and colleagues. Sadly, however, Simon's marriage has not survived his transformation: "My wife found it hard to cope with. One of my sons told me, 'Mummy can't get her head around it.' She told me that she couldn't deal with this as well as the kids, and we ended up separating. She always wanted me to change, but I changed in a way she didn't expect."

In fact, the breakdown of marriages and relationships is not uncommon in the aftermath of TTT. After such a radical change, it's not surprising that a gulf may open up between shifters and their partners, relatives, and old friends. After all, spiritual awakening means taking on a new identity. Although some personality traits may remain, shifters essentially become different people who just happen to live in the same body. So the partners of shifters suddenly find that they are no longer with the same person. They find themselves living with a person they don't understand, someone with different values and attitudes and who sees the world in a completely different way. Their partner may be undergoing confusing and disturbing experiences, which they are unable to help them with. In some cases, they are able to adjust, but these issues often place a great strain on relationships.

TTT and the Disappearance of Illness

Parker used the phrase "flipping a drastic switch" to describe his transformation, which is a perfect analogy for sudden and dramatic

TTT. If you remember, Adrian used almost the same phrase — "like the flick of a switch" — in chapter 3 to describe his transformation in prison. And the fact that the shift happened while both Parker and Simon were asleep emphasizes that it can occur without any expectation or volition. This also makes it clear that sudden TTT is a real and identifiable psychological event, as discrete and tangible as a physical change to the body.

Interestingly, Parker's and Simon's stories suggest a connection between TTT and illness. They both reported that, after their shifts, they became free of physical ailments. Parker said he was no longer bothered by the lower back pain that he had suffered from for months, while Simon described becoming free of a digestive complaint that had plagued him for fifteen years. These changes may sound mysterious, but they can be explained in terms of the shifters' new identity. Since the mind and body are so closely interconnected, the mind can both generate and alleviate illnesses and ailments. (In particular, digestive problems are known to be strongly psychosomatic.) So it's perhaps not surprising that, with the arising of a new identity and a new mind, the ailments that were produced by the *old* identities of Parker and Simon should fade away.

There is a link here with Parker's story of his initial spiritual awakening, when he woke up and suddenly found himself free of his drug addiction. This also seems mysterious. As Parker's psychiatrist wondered, how is it possible for a serious drug addiction to suddenly disappear overnight?

This leads us into the next chapter, where we look at TTT specifically in the context of addiction. This will also involve looking more deeply at the connection between suicidal intentions and spiritual awakening.

7

RELEASE FROM CRAVING

Transformation through Addiction

In chapter 1 I mentioned Russel Williams, who underwent a spiritual awakening after many years of suffering and later became a spiritual teacher based in my home city — Manchester, England. Amazed to find that there was an intensely awakened person living and teaching so close to me, I attended Russel's meetings regularly for more than twenty years and eventually helped him to write a book about his life and teachings (called *Not I, Not Other Than I: The Spiritual Teachings of Russel Williams*).

Russel was ninety-three when the book was published, which probably makes him the world's oldest first-time author! At that time, he was holding public meetings every Monday and Wednesday evening — in fact, he continued to do so until a few weeks before his death three years later, in 2018. The meetings were open to anyone and free of charge and became very popular after the book's publication. People began to travel from far afield to attend them, sometimes even from the United States or Israel.

One evening I met two young men who had traveled down from Scotland to see Russel. They didn't look at all like the typical attendees of Russel's meetings. Aside from being so young — perhaps in their late twenties — they looked like normal working-class lads, with short hair and fashionable, sporty clothes.

At a break in the meeting, I chatted with one of them (we will call him Greg). He told me that he and his friend were both recovering drug addicts who had met at a Narcotics Anonymous group. After years of addiction, heroin had taken such a strong hold over him that he had given up hope of stopping and was resigned to dying. But one morning he woke up and felt completely different. He had no idea why, but he suddenly felt clearheaded and strong. Normally the first thing he thought of when he got up was taking drugs, but that morning the urge had disappeared. The thought of taking heroin repulsed him. For no apparent reason, he felt free of his addiction. He felt a sense of wholeness and ease that he had not known since he was a child.

"I knew it was over," he told me. "I didn't want to be around my drug-taking friends anymore. I didn't have anything in common with them. They couldn't relate to me, couldn't understand why I'd changed so suddenly. It was the same with my family. All my relationships ended or changed because I wasn't the same person anymore. I had to find a whole new set of friends based on the different person I had become."

Greg didn't know anything about spirituality, but after attending some Narcotics Anonymous meetings, he began to realize that he had undergone a spiritual transformation. He began to read spiritual books and watch videos of talks by spiritual teachers, building up a framework to make sense of what had happened to him. His visits to Russel were part of the process of understanding and exploring his transformation.

Of course, we saw another example of this phenomenon in the last chapter: Parker, who woke up after a week-long drug binge to find that his addiction had mysteriously disappeared, for no apparent reason. I call this phenomenon "addiction release," and it is one of the most striking — and least studied — effects of sudden spiritual awakening.

It seems almost incredible. How can someone wake up in the morning and simply find that they are no longer an addict? How can a severe addiction suddenly disappear for no apparent reason? Overcoming addiction is often a long struggle. Recovering addicts usually have to proceed carefully, on a day-by-day basis, with a lot of support and personal courage to keep themselves from relapsing.

But this is not always the case. When addiction is at its most extreme — when a person has lost everything and is close to death — then the strange phenomenon of addiction release may occur. The old self that was burdened with the addiction dies, and a new self takes its place. And since the new self has just been born and doesn't carry any attachments or influences from the past, it is free of the addiction. Strictly speaking, although it may appear that an addiction has suddenly dropped away from a person, what has actually happened is that — equally miraculously — the person who was an addict no longer exists. It is not the addiction that has disappeared, but the person.

It's worth noting that one of the founders of Alcoholics Anonymous, Bill Wilson, underwent this experience himself. After relapsing more times than he could count, Wilson felt completely broken down by his alcoholism and was close to insanity and death. After checking in to a New York hospital, he was in bed racked with physical pain and mental torment, when an awakening occurred: "My room blazed with an indescribably white light. I was seized with an ecstasy beyond description.... I lay on the shores of a new world."[1]

Because of his experience, Wilson believed that recovery from alcoholism was only possible through spiritual transformation. And he developed the AA 12-step program as a way of helping other alcoholics to undergo awakening. (The final step of the AA program reads, "Having had a spiritual awakening as the result of these steps, we tried to carry this message to alcoholics and to practice these principles in all our affairs.") You might say that the program is an attempt to *gradually* cultivate the same transformation that Wilson went through *instantaneously*. As such, the AA 12-step process is essentially a path of spiritual development, along similar lines to the eightfold path of Buddhism or the eight-limbed path of yoga.[2]

Albert Einstein reputedly stated that a problem cannot be solved from the same mindset that created it, and this applies to addiction. In order to be free of addiction, the ego-self that has been taken over by the addiction has to dissolve away. If anything remains of that ego-self, then the addiction — and the craving for the substance — will remain. To paraphrase Einstein, an addiction cannot be overcome by the same self that carries the addiction. It can only be overcome by a new self.

As with spiritual awakening in general, this process can occur both gradually and suddenly, and at varying degrees of intensity. In this chapter, we're going to look at two cases in which addiction release occurred in the midst of sudden and intense awakening.

Addiction and Trauma

The practice of ingesting consciousness-altering substances is thousands of years old. Traces of drugs like opium and cannabis have been found in ancient European sites dating back six thousand years. Many of the world's indigenous peoples also have traditions of using consciousness-altering substances. American Indian tribes have sacred plants such as peyote and fly agaric mushrooms, while the tribes of the Amazon use substances such as ayahuasca. As the United States found out during Prohibition, the human need for consciousness-altering substances is so powerful that it seems impossible to regulate or suppress.

In some cases, drugs are taken for transcendental reasons — to expand the parameters of our awareness and give us access to a more intense and expansive reality normally hidden from us. This is the main motive for taking psychedelics such as LSD and ayahuasca. Indigenous cultures have primarily used drugs for transcendental reasons, which is why they were usually associated with ceremonies or rituals or used specifically by shamans.

But probably the most common reason for human beings to take drugs is to deal with psychological discord — to escape boredom or a general sense of frustration or discontent due to a lack of meaning, purpose, or hope. Some drugs work by anesthetizing us to our psychological discord, while others work by creating positive feelings that override the discord. Heroin is the best example of the first type of drug, while cocaine is a good example of the second. Sadly, the main use of drugs by some contemporary indigenous groups is no longer for transcendental but for escapist reasons, in response to the trauma of cultural destruction and a loss of purpose and meaning.

Generally, the more severe a person's psychological discord, the more likely they are to use drugs, and the more likely they are to become an addict. When psychological discord is intense, there is also a tendency to use pain-numbing drugs rather than stimulants. In fact, research has shown a clear relationship between addiction and trauma — particularly, childhood trauma such as sexual or physical abuse. One study of 470 drug or alcohol addicts found that 81 percent of women and 69 percent of men had suffered sexual abuse during childhood.[3] Alcohol and drugs are a way of numbing the pain of trauma, with its symptoms of self-hatred, anxiety, and suspicion.

It's difficult to make a clear distinction between transformation through addiction and the depression-related awakenings described in the last chapter. Both types of awakening originate in psychological discord; the only difference is that addicts go through a long process of attempting to manage their discord by taking drugs. Ultimately, though, this just leads to more discord — more depression, more self-hatred, and more loss. The ego-dissolving effects of psychological turmoil are intensified by addiction, which makes breakdown more likely. This is why — like imprisonment, bereavement, and facing death — addiction holds a high degree of spiritual potential, since a breakdown may also mean a shift up.

"Everything Comes from the One Life, the Same Source" — Nikki's Story

Nikki Phelan is in her early fifties and helps to run a retreat in the Yorkshire countryside. The retreat has its roots in Christian principles. Once Christianity was Nikki's only point of reference, so when she had a spiritual awakening, she interpreted it in Christian terms. Later, she began to realize that her experience went beyond religion, concepts, or doctrines. Nikki told me that she feels she has actually experienced two spiritual awakenings. The first, most profound awakening happened while she was in rehab after ten years of drug addiction and mental illness.

Nikki had a happy childhood, until she was abused by the family doctor at the age of thirteen:

That was the first thing that seemed to set me off course. I didn't know what was going on or how to process it. I felt ashamed and under threat as a person. It started a pattern of looking to older men to protect me, since I felt so vulnerable. Then I changed schools and was bullied and started drinking, trying to fit in. I had a boyfriend who was older and protected me from the bullying. I felt like I needed protection from the world. He was a nice guy who did his best to look after me, and I clung to him for safety and protection. I was pregnant at sixteen and married at seventeen. I had my first son, but I wasn't there emotionally. I was really still a child myself.

I left my husband and met someone else and had another son. My new boyfriend was a big, older guy who I was sure would be able to protect me, but that relationship didn't work out either. I ended up on my own with two small children in quite a notorious council estate in Bradford. I felt completely out of my depth. I felt I was born as one of those people who just could not cope with life. I literally did not have a clue what was going on.

One of the main things I took my sense of identity from and had a big attachment to was my appearance. I did some modeling when I was younger, which wasn't good because I was actually really insecure. I would spend hours doing my makeup and hair and wouldn't go out of the house until I thought I looked perfect. If I didn't get the attention I craved, I would go home and redo my whole appearance.

I ended up attracting another guy who I thought could protect me, but he was in a dark place, although I couldn't see it at the time. Something terrible happened, and both my children were taken from me and went to live with my mum and dad full-time. This event was another big catalyst for my life spiraling downward. I felt deep shame and guilt since, ultimately, I felt it was my fault. I started developing the thought that I was evil. I hated myself. The idea that I was evil kept growing and growing.

This was in the early 1990s, when the rave scene was growing in Bradford. Up to this point, I had been really antidrugs, but because I was feeling so confused and I was going around with people who were taking drugs, it became more and more familiar. I started taking party drugs, like speed and Ecstasy. They did their job in the beginning, helping me to escape myself and reality. That went on for a couple of years, taking more and more drugs, but eventually they stopped working, as they do when you get used to them. I was going out nearly every night, and my brain was becoming more and more fried. The group I was going around with said, "Oh, you should smoke this – it helps you to come down." I was so naive, I thought I was smoking marijuana, but actually it was heroin. So I started smoking heroin without even realizing it. I never knew you could smoke it. I had always associated heroin with needles and injecting.

One day my boyfriend at the time came around, and I had this horrible flu. I couldn't get out of bed. And my boyfriend said,

"Well, you're rattling – you know, withdrawing from heroin." And I said, "Who's been taking heroin?" "You have." You'd think in that moment I would have stopped, but I didn't, because I felt so ill and because when I wasn't under the influence of drugs, all the bad memories, thoughts, and feelings of guilt and shame came flooding back.

That became ten years of living in hell. I also developed a crack habit and an addiction to prescription medication. I had two nervous breakdowns in that time, and my mental health got worse and worse because of all the drugs I was taking. It was as if a black cloud was always following me around. I was split in two – the real me and another entity that seemed to take over more and more. It felt like they were at war with each other all the time.

I started to hear a voice that was external to me. At one point I couldn't go to the bathroom because I heard this voice telling me to kill myself. I wouldn't go out of the house. I used to hide and lock myself in cupboards because I could hear noises all around the house. One time I was sectioned [committed] and put on medication for schizophrenia. For weeks, I had no idea where I was. They said that my brain had shut down to protect itself. Following that I was on heavy medication. I hid behind the label of being mentally ill so I didn't have to deal with life.

I kept trying to come off drugs, but it didn't last long, and I ended up going from bad to worse. I stole lots of money from my dad, and he had me arrested in the hope it might jerk me out of the cycle I was in. Despite it all, my mum and dad and my family – including my boys – continued to love me and tried to help me. I was on more and more medication and sleeping most of the time. The only time I went out of the house was once a week, with my boyfriend to get my script from the doctor.

Not long after this I decided I just couldn't go on living in the hell in my own mind, so I decided to kill myself. I had tried to take my own life a couple of times before, more as a cry for help or attention, but this time I meant it. I had such a feeling of peace about it. I spent a week planning it, making sure I had enough tablets. I felt happy that finally there was a way out.

So when the day came, I had all the tablets lined up and I was getting ready to do it. I wasn't scared at all. I was beyond fear, since I was just so desperate. But somewhere in the corner of my bedroom there was a tiny passport-size photo of my two kids, and it fell on the floor. I looked at this tiny picture of my boys and it snapped me out of it. I threw myself on the floor and said, "God – if you really exist, if you really are real, please help me, or I'm going to die." I knew in that moment that my only hope was if there was something other than myself.

Two doors down from me there happened to live a woman who worked for a drug organization, helping people. I went and stood at my window, watching for her to come home from work. As soon as she got through her front door, I went around and literally threw myself on the floor at her feet, saying, "Sue – please help me, or I am literally going to die." She told me later she could tell I genuinely wanted help.

Two weeks later I was in rehab, with unconditional funding for as long as I needed. That was rare – most people only got full funding for the initial detox period.

Nikki's spiritual awakening occurred a few weeks after she started rehab. After six weeks of detox, she started to have more in-depth therapy, which she had to engage with as part of her program. Although she was healing physically, she was still fragile psychologically. One part of the program was a parenting class, and she was terrified of going, because she knew she would have to confront her guilt and sadness about her children. Her awakening happened the night before she was due to go to the class:

Everything in me wanted to leave, since I knew what was coming the next day in that parenting class. I wanted to run and use drugs to numb the pain and the fear. But I knew that trying to escape from myself was a losing battle. Everywhere I went, there I was. Even the drugs didn't work in the end. I was literally clinging on to a bench to stop myself from leaving, and I remember saying to myself, "I'm not going to leave. I don't know what it is I need to do, but I'm not going to leave."

I walked up to my room and threw myself on the floor. There was just nowhere else to go. I had completely run out of options. I decided that I wasn't going to leave, and I wasn't going to use. The only thing I could do was to get down on my hands and knees and pray.

A feeling of peace rose inside me and literally covered me. It was an actual tangible peace. I heard a voice from within, and I just knew in an instant that I was forgiven, that I was accepted, and that I was loved. I was filled with the most overwhelming sense of love, even for myself. It was massive because I had hated myself so much. Before rehab I had turned around every mirror in the house because I despised myself so much. I genuinely thought I saw an evil person looking back at me. But now I just felt this overwhelming love for myself and for everybody else. I had gone from darkness into the light. I was literally a new person in an instant. The weight of the world had been lifted off my shoulders, and I felt light and free.

I saw my counselor later that night, and he noticed how much I had changed in the few short hours since he'd last seen me. Weeks later, he told me that he'd never seen someone go upstairs as one person and come back down a completely different person. I was singing and dancing and felt like I was floating on air. I was experiencing a spiritual realm that I knew absolutely nothing about.

The desire to take heroin and escape from myself was gone. I felt liberated but most of all deeply loved and accepted, with this overwhelming sense of love for the world and myself. After the awakening, I remember walking around for months as if I was floating on air. It was so much better than any Ecstasy tablet or drug I had ever taken, because it was real joy. I saw the world through fresh eyes and could sense people's auras, their light or density. I didn't have a clue what had happened to me or know anyone else it had happened to.

I used to spend hours in my room just speaking to God and going within. I wasn't scared of myself anymore. I didn't know what to expect, but I just knew that I'd be okay no matter what. I would literally spend hours and hours in my room, just sitting there observing whatever feelings came up, wrapped in the safety of the love that I felt. I couldn't identify with the person I was before. That person had been very insecure, jealous, and self-centered. Not a nice person at all. But now I just felt love and the deep urge to help other people.

Nikki's only way of making any sense of her experience was through Christianity. Since she felt she had been born again, she identified herself as a born-again Christian. Her youngest son came to live with her, and soon afterward she moved back to Yorkshire, where she became heavily involved in a church she had occasionally attended earlier, during her addiction. She helped to lead a women's ministry with a friend named Cath, who had befriended her when she was still involved with drugs.

Gradually, however, Nikki started to feel that something wasn't right. She felt restricted and exhausted. She had become so busy with church activities that she had stopped going inward. She felt a need to detach herself from the church, until she left altogether. However, without the support of the church, she felt isolated and vulnerable. There were difficulties in her family, and she went through a period of confusion. As she understands it now, she had lost touch with her authentic self — her awakened self — as a result of misinterpreting her experiences and becoming too focused on the external, conditioned aspects of religion.

However, Nikki had the chance to move out into the countryside, where the open space and quietness helped her to reconnect and go within again. She started to read other spiritual literature, rather than specifically Christian books, and realized that she had to put her own spiritual journey first again, without the restrictions of organized religion. This was Nikki's second awakening: a gradual process of regaining contact with the new awakened self that had been born seventeen years earlier. She finally established an authentic framework to make sense of her experiences:

> At first I thought I was being blasphemous, but in the depths of my being I knew it was right. I had a moment of clarity. I knew I had to let go of everything, including my own concepts and beliefs. I had to align myself with my spiritual path and continue with my inner journey. From that point on, it was a gradual awakening, day by day. It was a process of coming back to my true self.
>
> Now I feel like I've woken up from a dream. I realize now that the dark cloud that used to follow me around was the dark cloud of thoughts. The realization that I am not my thoughts was one of my most liberating experiences. Now the clouds of my thoughts may come, but I can just watch them pass by, without logging in and identifying with them and making them personal. Because of this I feel that I'm the real me and have such a deep peace and contentment. I don't have any desire to do or be anything in particular. I'm just content in being. I sense that I'm in the natural flow of life. It feels like the quest is over and there's nothing to seek anymore. I am home. I feel so deeply thankful.
>
> I used to think of God as a separate entity but now I feel that there is no separation between me and God. We are one. Everything comes from the one life, the same source.

As well as being an amazing tale of spiritual transformation — the birth of a new self from the ashes of an old, shattered ego — Nikki's story underlines the importance of having an authentic framework to make sense of a spiritual transformation. Nikki used a Christian framework to try to make sense of it, which eventually led to confusion and alienation from her awakened self. The confusion was only superficial but created a barrier that took a long time to overcome.

Nikki's story emphasizes that spiritual awakening is not the end of the journey, but the beginning of a different journey. Awakening is often a challenging process of adjustment and integration, requiring self-understanding and self-acceptance. However, as discussed previously, in almost every case I am aware of, awakenings do become integrated eventually, even if it takes several years.

"My Whole Psyche Changed Completely" – Eve's Story

There are no rigid rules about spiritual awakening — only patterns that occur in most cases. While most people (like Nikki and Donna in the last chapter) go through a long period of adjustment after transformation, others (like Parker) seem to sail through the process without any turbulence. The story we're going to read now is a good example of this. At the same time, Eve's story is the most striking example of sudden release from addiction that I have come across — and one of the most amazing stories of TTT in general that I have investigated.[4]

Eve is a forty-eight-year-old woman from Edinburgh, Scotland, who is bright, cheerful, and glowing with health and vitality. She runs a company that organizes conferences and other events for businesses. If you met her, you would find it difficult to imagine that, until nine years ago, she lived a life of incredible chaos and suffering. At the same time, it's not necessary to compare her present life to her previous one, because in a very real sense she is not the same person who led that previous life.

Another way in which Eve's story breaks the normal pattern is that, unlike many addicts, she didn't have an abusive childhood. She came from a stable background, with parents who were attentive and caring and had high moral standards. Her parents didn't smoke or drink and had a harmonious marriage. Her other siblings did well at school and college and entered middle-class professions and had stable and successful lives. Eve can't pinpoint any reason why her life turned out so differently from theirs, or why she became an alcoholic. As she says, "It just seemed to be inside me."

When Eve was five or six, her behavior started to become

wayward. She would steal cigarettes from her grandmother and smoke them and also steal money from her mother's or grandmother's purse. She became disruptive at school and was forced to sit separately from the other kids. At the age of ten, she was suspended from primary school for a week for sitting in the staff room and smoking one of the teacher's cigarettes:

> I don't know why I was doing these things. But somehow it was all fear-based. I had a feeling of being really separate from everyone in my family and from the other kids at school. I always felt on the outside looking in, totally disconnected and isolated. I didn't feel like I fitted in or that I knew what I was doing. Everybody else seemed to know what they were doing.

Eve started to drink when she was nine or ten years old. Although they didn't drink, her parents had a drinks cabinet for guests, and Eve would mix different spirits together in a flask, which she hid in her bedroom. She drank from the flask before going to school in the morning, because it took her fear away. At the age of thirteen she would drink in the park with her friends in the evenings, but whereas they had a cut-off point, she didn't seem to get as drunk as they did and always wanted more.

Eve left school at fifteen and took a job as a trainee chef. There was a culture of heavy drinking among the other chefs, and she drank all the time when she wasn't working, drinking during the afternoon breaks between her shifts and at the end of her evening shift. She was already a full-fledged alcoholic. She started to have blackouts and became involved in dangerous situations. As Eve says, "I was waking up in shady places with shady people who were older than me, and I couldn't remember what had happened. I became promiscuous by proxy, going home with people because they had booze and I could carry on drinking. It wrecked my self-esteem even more, and it all led to another drink, because drinking would stop me feeling so bad about myself."

At the age of eighteen, Eve inherited some money when her grandmother died. Her parents decided she should go abroad, to separate her from the heavy drinkers she was hanging around with. But the plan had the opposite effect. She flew to Italy and quickly found work in a bar. Drinks were free for bar workers, and as Eve says, "I was absolutely legless for a couple of years. My behavior was awful. I thought that people who had families and went to the cinema were losers. I thought I was just open-minded and liberal and everyone else was boring."

Eve had an American boyfriend who managed the bar where she was working. When he decided to return to the States, she went along with him. But the relationship didn't work out, and she ended up living in a trailer park:

Most of the people at the trailer park had higher moral standards than me. I was morally bankrupt, and my behavior became even more bizarre. I was never sober. I took drugs too. I would take whatever was going – I wouldn't even ask what it was until two minutes afterward. But drugs were always secondary to alcohol. Once I sniffed some heroin, and hours later when I came to, I saw an unopened bottle of lager on the coffee table. And I thought, "This is no good. Drugs are getting in the way of alcohol."

I was addicted to drama as well as alcohol. You get yourself in so much trouble in a blackout or on a bender. I wasn't capable of making sensible conscious decisions. All my decisions were awful and dangerous, and they all revolved around alcohol. My survival instinct was secondary to my obsession with alcohol. I ended up in so many dangerous situations. I was raped so many times over the years and had a lot of other violent encounters. I never reported them because I thought I was worthless and so it didn't matter.

Eventually Eve was deported from the US, and over the next few years she drifted around the UK, from city to city and job to job. As she told me, "I would move somewhere and I could put on a good front. People would think I was good fun. It didn't take them long to suss me out. I would lie to them and steal from them."

Eve was arrested for drunk driving and banned from driving for fifteen years but carried on driving anyway. She did community service, had counseling, and attended drug and alcohol awareness courses but had no intention of stopping drinking. Even when her physical health started to deteriorate, it didn't change her behavior. She went to the hospital with a kidney infection and was told that her liver was three times the normal size. On leaving the hospital, she went straight to the pub.

Eve had further encounters with violent men. One man strangled her in a passageway and probably would have killed her if he hadn't been disturbed by passers-by. On another occasion, she was taken hostage by a convicted murderer but managed to escape after several days. Again, she didn't go to the police because she felt that she deserved to be treated so brutally.

Eventually Eve was drinking ten to twelve bottles of wine a day — she drank wine because she thought it looked more socially acceptable. She would drink on an empty stomach as soon as she woke up in the morning. But by this point the alcohol wasn't working anymore. She was drinking just to stop herself from shaking and having alcoholic fits. If she went more than forty-five minutes without a drink, feelings of terror and paranoia would overwhelm her. She was having hallucinations and sensing evil presences around her.

Below Eve tells the story of the final stages of her breakdown and of the incredible transformation that occurred afterward:

I ended up homeless because I'd burned all my bridges. My family tried everything. I was institutionalized, but I ran away, jumped over the fence. Nothing worked. I just wanted to drink. I used to phone the Samaritans and cry my eyes out for hours and hours. By that point the party was over.

All my relationships were ruined. I was just wandering the streets. In a strange way it was the easiest time because I had completely given up on myself. It was just carefree drinking. I didn't have to try and hide it, so I could drink openly on the streets.

It came to an end when I tried to commit suicide. It wasn't a cry for help. The alcohol had stopped working, and I was completely broken down, physically and emotionally and spiritually. Whenever I woke up from my drunken stupor, I was disappointed that I was still alive. There was a feeling of dread – "Oh God, I'm still alive. How am I going to get through today?" I was a wreck, an empty shell. I'd walk a few steps and then have to stop and sit down or lie down on the pavement. I had nothing to live for, nothing to give, and I thought, "I can't do this anymore. I don't have the strength. Even when I do have a drink it doesn't last more than an hour before the paranoia and hallucinations start."

I walked in front of a bus that was traveling at 40 miles an hour. I genuinely wanted the bus to hit me, but it swerved. The police were called, and I thought they were going to arrest me, but the policeman wanted to help. He asked me, "What are you doing to yourself? What are you doing to your life? Is there nobody we can get in touch with? Is there nowhere you can go?"

I hadn't spoken to my parents in quite a while. It was too much for them – I was breaking their hearts. But I told the policeman to phone them, and he took me back to my mum and dad's.

This was when the miracle occurred. My mum said, "I suppose I'll have to give you alcohol," and I said yes. She gave me some red wine and I desperately needed it. I was rattling, in withdrawal. I picked up the glass, lifted it, then put it down. I kept picking it up and putting it down. It wasn't me that was putting it down. It was such a strange phenomenon. I was like, "I need this drink," then the hand would just put it down.

The doctor knocked me out for a few days, and when I came to, I didn't want to drink. For as long as I can remember, I had thought about drinking every single second of every day. It was all about the next drink, about where it was coming from. But now it had just gone.

When I came to, Mum sat me down in front of a mirror, and said, "Look at yourself, you're an alcoholic." I was thirty-nine years old. I looked at myself, and it was one of the most surreal experiences I've ever had. I had no idea who I was. I didn't connect with my reflection. It could have been a completely different person. It felt like a completely different person. I said to my mum, "Who is that?" And she said, "It's you." And I said, "No, it's not – I don't recognize that person."

It was such a strange phenomenon. I didn't make any decisions. I didn't do anything. But the need, the want, just disappeared. I'm involved with AA now, and we always say that people have to change their behavior. But I didn't change anything. My behavior just changed. I just changed, like magic. One day I was a person who would lie and steal and do anything. And now I'd changed into this person who was honest and kind. My mum said it was as if I'd had a psychic change, as if my whole personality had changed. And that was how it felt.

Nine years later, Eve has still not touched a drop of alcohol or felt the urge to drink. Working in AA, she is fully aware that a lot of people struggle to stay sober, but she never has. As she says, "I feel really bad for people who are struggling, but I never have. Even when I went through hard times, like when I lost my mum, I never once thought about drinking again."

Eve was slightly confused by her transformation at first, but soon it settled down, and she began to feel liberated and elated. She had powerful experiences when, in her words, "I felt super connected to everything." At the time she didn't know anything about spirituality but began to learn about it through AA meetings and realized that her transformation could be explained in spiritual terms. In fact, other AA members informed her that she had had a spiritual awakening. People told her later that when she first came to her AA group, she looked so ill and broken down that they thought she was going to die and that they had never seen such a major shift as hers.

Reflecting on the amazing shift she had undergone, Eve told me:

We all have ups and downs — I suffered the loss of my mum a few years ago, and I adored her; she was my life. But I can honestly say that compared to the life that I had before, I've never really had a bad day. I just feel light. I feel full of gratitude. That sense of elation and liberation has never really left me. I live a simple, quiet life. I notice the small things and I really appreciate them. At first people told me, "You're on a pink cloud. It'll only last for a wee while; you'll come off it soon." And I said, "No, I'm not. I'm staying up here, thanks very much." And I did!

It was such a relief that I didn't have to lie anymore. It was such a relief that I wasn't afraid anymore. I don't worry about anything. I have a sense of inner trust. My whole psyche changed completely. I have no trauma, in spite of all the terrible things I went through. And I don't feel any hatred toward the people who did those things to me. I find it easy to forgive. I don't want to carry around a big suitcase of regret. A lot of people struggle through the AA steps because they don't want to go back and reflect. They find it too painful. But I just lapped it all up. I threw myself into it. And now the main thing in my life is to try to help others, especially other alcoholics.

It was like being catapulted from one world into the next. Something — a higher power, the universe, God, whatever it is — took this obsession away from me and made me sober for a reason.

Freedom from Addiction and Trauma

One of the most interesting aspects of Eve's story is that when her mother asked her to look in the mirror, she didn't recognize herself. This is a very clear illustration of the shift in identity that takes place in sudden spiritual awakening or TTT. Shortly after her suicide attempt, Eve's old identity dissolved away and a new identity took its place. This was also evident in the strange experience she had when she lifted up a glass of wine and immediately put it down again, saying, "It wasn't me that was putting it down."

Like Nikki and Parker from the last chapter, Eve describes how the urge to drink left her suddenly and completely, never to return. In nine years, she has never had any struggle remaining sober. As Eve says, this is in marked contrast to most alcoholics and addicts, who face a daily struggle to stay sober. Nikki said the same of her transformation. Since her moment of awakening, she has never had any desire to take drugs. Nikki told me that, during her rehab sessions, she didn't feel comfortable standing up and saying, "My name's Nikki, and I'm an addict," because she felt free of her addiction. Instead, she would stand up and say, "My name's Nikki, and I am free!"

In a similar story to Eve's, a woman named Amber told me how her alcoholism led to two suicide attempts, culminating in an instant awakening that she described as "monumental and miraculous." And with the awakening there was a sudden "cessation of the desire to drink." These days Amber works in the restaurant industry and has to serve alcohol every day. As she told me, "I serve it. I mix drinks. I must smell the wine I decant tableside for any defects, and I have zero craving. This all happened instantly and before I even entered an AA room."

Like Nikki, Amber is puzzled by the fact that she somehow managed to overcome alcoholism effortlessly, without support, whereas most people she encounters in AA groups struggle for years to stay sober. Now, three years after her shift, she says that she lives in a "world of gratitude, fearlessness, hope, love, happiness, and acceptance. All I've ever wanted was to feel normal and happy and to be free, and now I feel like I have all that."

Addiction release is certainly a kind of miracle, and it is surely a phenomenon that needs more investigation. At the same time, it is a miracle that can be explained, at least to a degree. You might recall that in the last chapter, Parker's psychiatrist suggested that the disappearance of his addiction was due to some chemical change in the frontal lobes of his brain, which controls desire and craving. However, it's much more likely that the change is due to psycho-spiritual factors rather than chemical ones.

In TTT death and birth occur. There is the death of one identity and the birth of another: the death of the ego and its replacement by a latent, higher-functioning awakened self. The deceased ego carried the person's addiction to drugs or alcohol, whereas the new self that has been born has no addictions. How could it, since it has only just come into being? In other words, in these cases it is not so much the addiction that disappears but the self that was addicted. Amber told me that, although she survived her suicide attempts, she feels that she actually *did* die. And in a psychological sense this is completely accurate.

Another intriguing aspect of Nikki's and Eve's transformations is how they both became free of the effects of previous trauma. Eve described this very clearly, telling me, "I have no trauma, in spite of all the terrible things I went through." It is remarkable that, after going through such extreme experiences of violence and abuse — in Eve's case, thirty years of horrendous experiences, including multiple rapes and other violent encounters — they are both apparently free of anxiety, guilt, and other symptoms of post-traumatic stress disorder. In fact, both Nikki and Eve have an extremely high level of psychological health.

As with addiction (and the disappearance of Parker's and Simon's physical ailments), the only way to account for this freedom from trauma is in terms of the birth of a new identity. Nikki's and Eve's trauma passed away with their old identity, along with their addictions. Their new identity doesn't carry any effects of their trauma. Why should it, since it is a new self that has no past and no previous experiences? (We will discuss this release from trauma in more detail in the next chapter, since it doesn't just apply to transformation through addiction but to TTT in general.)

In this way, transformation through addiction is very significant, since it clearly illustrates the central theme of this book: how a person's ego-identity can dissolve away and be replaced by a latent, higher-functioning, awakened self. In cases such as Nikki's and Eve's, we see the differences between these two selves clearly, in the emergence of a new self that is free of the addiction and the trauma that blighted the old self.

This leads us to the next chapter, in which we move beyond descriptions of the shifters' experiences and into an explanation of them.

8

EXPLAINING TRANSFORMATION
THROUGH TURMOIL

love the idea that some phenomena are simply mysterious or magical and that there's no point trying to explain them. I enjoy reading about quantum physics because it seems to defy any logical explanation. Particles are linked together, even though they are miles apart; particles pop in and out of existence; they can be anywhere and nowhere at the same time; they can be waves and particles at the same time.

Some authors have suggested that spiritual experiences are beyond explanation too. The psychologist Abraham Maslow believed that what he called "peak experiences" — moments of ecstatic happiness — are spontaneous and mysterious and that there is nothing we can do to generate them.[1] However, although transformation through turmoil is certainly miraculous, I don't think it is wholly mysterious. I believe that — to an extent, at least — it can be explained. In this chapter, I will offer my explanation.

But before I do that, I would like to briefly highlight some of the main points that have emerged from this book. As I mentioned in the introduction, I found it incredibly inspiring to interview the shifters featured in this book. Even when I reread stories such as

Eve's and Donna's, I feel moved to tears. I find it amazing that they experienced such extreme suffering and emerged not just unscathed but liberated and transformed, reborn as higher-functioning, awakened human beings.

At the same time, I find the shifters' experiences fascinating from an academic point of view. They have made me aware of certain aspects of TTT that weren't as evident from my previous research. I've touched on a few of these aspects already — particularly in the last two chapters — but I think it would be useful to emphasize them and to bring them together.

The Disappearance of Addiction, Trauma, and Illness

Although it sometimes occurs gradually, it is most common for TTT to occur instantaneously, as a sudden shift in identity. The person's old ego breaks down or dissolves away, and a new identity emerges to take its place. This new identity is completely different from the person's previous identity, so that the shifter often feels as if they are a different person living in the same body. Some superficial personality traits remain, and people retain the memories associated with their previous identity (even if they don't directly associate themselves with them). But the essence of their identity is completely different. Shifters have a new perception of the world, new values (such as becoming less materialistic and more altruistic), new kinds of relationships, a new relationship to time (i.e., they are more focused on the present and less oriented toward the past and future), and so on.

In the last chapter, I touched on other interesting ways in which this identity shift can manifest. First, we discussed the phenomenon of addiction release, when the old self that was carrying the addiction dies away and is replaced by a new self that doesn't carry it. In theory, addiction release should occur in every case of addiction-related TTT (certainly when TTT occurs suddenly and dramatically). This is an area that I'm looking forward to investigating further in the future.

Second, I discussed the phenomenon of the disappearance of past trauma. This happened to Nikki and Eve but also to several of the other shifters in this book who went through intense trauma. For example, Ananta's three years of extreme hardship and suffering in a Japanese prison, as described in chapter 3, have apparently left no traumatic aftereffects. Donna from chapter 6 has also become free of the childhood trauma that caused her depression and psychological discord. As with addiction, we can account for this only in terms of the emergence of a new self. The old self that carried the trauma dissolved away, and a new self was born, free from trauma. As with addiction, why should the newborn self carry any trauma, since it has no past and no previous experiences?

A third way in which the radical identity shift of TTT manifests is through the sudden disappearance of physical ailments. We saw examples of this in chapter 6, when Simon remarked that his digestive problems instantly disappeared and Parker reported that his chronic back pain abated. Again, this can be explained in terms of the death of an old identity and the birth of a new one. It is well known that many physical ailments and illnesses are psychosomatic — that is, caused (or exacerbated) by psychological factors such as stress, worry, depression, or the repression of traumatic experiences. When TTT occurs, these psychological traits evaporate along with the ego, and so the physical ailments that they caused evaporate too. This is another area I would love to investigate in more detail. It would be interesting to discover how common this experience is in TTT. Not all illnesses and ailments are psychosomatic, so it may not be a phenomenon that occurs across the board.[2]

It's difficult to say for sure, but it appears that these effects occur when TTT is gradual too. In chapter 1, we read about the gradual transformation of three soldiers — Gus, Gary, and David. In particular, Gus and David experienced severe PTSD, which faded away as they underwent gradual awakening.

New Self, Not No-Self

In *The Leap* I argued against the notion that spiritual awakening is a state of no-self, as some spiritual teachers and traditions suggest. Strictly speaking, wakefulness is a state of *new* self, a fact that has been borne out by the findings of this book.

Let me use the analogy of a house. When TTT occurs, it's like a house suddenly collapsing (or in the case of gradual TTT, being dismantled slowly). But in TTT when an old house disappears, it doesn't just leave an empty plot of land. A new structure emerges in its place. If there was just an empty space of no-self, a person wouldn't be able to function in the world. Without psychological structures or a sense of identity, they would be unable to concentrate, to retain information, to make plans, to organize their lives, to hold conversations. If there really was "no one there" inside them, just an empty space of experience, they would be in a state of psychosis. In some cases of TTT, it takes a while — sometimes several years — for the structures of the new house to become stable and well integrated. But eventually, once new psychological structures are in place, shifters find that they are able to function at a much high level than before.

In other words, the shifters featured in this book haven't become no one, they have become someone else. As I pointed out in *The Leap*, it's easy to mistake wakefulness for a state of no-self, because the awakened self is completely different from the old ego self. It is a much subtler and more labile kind of self, without a solid center. It is subtly interconnected with the world, without a sense of separation, and so it might appear as if there is "no one there." But all the same, the wakeful self has its own "self-system" of psychological structures and processes, including a sense of identity.

The Uniformity of the Wakeful State

The characteristics of the new self that emerges in TTT are remarkably uniform. All the people we've heard from in this book experience the world in essentially the same way. This is because they are experiencing the world through the same type of self-system, with the same type of psychological structures.

To continue the analogy, the house that human beings normally inhabit is a specific type of self-system consisting of specific psychological structures and processes. These generate a specific type of awareness and experience of reality that we often assume is objectively true, as if it's the only possible way that reality can be experienced. For example, two of the main features of our normal self-system are a familiarized, automatic perception of the world around us and a strong self-boundary that gives us a sense of being "located" inside our heads, in duality to the rest of the world.

Whenever someone undergoes a spiritual awakening, the same type of new self-system emerges inside them, with common psychological structures and processes. It's as if the new house that arises in TTT is based on the same architectural plans and made from the same materials. This self-system features a continual freshness and vividness of perception of our surroundings, instead of an automatic, familiarized perception. It doesn't have boundaries or a strong central point of location, so that it feels a sense of connection to — and participation in — the world rather than a sense of separation. In addition, it doesn't feature the constant chatter of an isolated and anxious ego-self. Thinking may still take place, but in a slower and quieter way, and without identification with thoughts. As a result, the self-system of wakefulness is a much more pleasant place to live than human beings' normal self-system.

In the appendix I highlight eighteen major characteristics of wakefulness, spread across (roughly) four areas: perceptual, affective, conceptual (or cognitive), and behavioral characteristics.

Although I don't have space to make a detailed analysis, I believe that a close reading of any the shifters' accounts over the last seven chapters would identify almost all (if not all) these characteristics. To take a few characteristics at random, all the shifters we've heard from have become less identified with their thoughts and less materialistic and more altruistic. They have all developed more intense perception, a greater sense of well-being, a sense of connection, a reduced fear of death, a greater sense of appreciation, and a wider sense of perspective; and they now have a greater enjoyment of quietness and solitude.

My previous research has also shown that in wakefulness people tend to experience all (or almost all) these characteristics, although some may be more prominent than others. The variation is usually due to personality traits — for example, a person who is more introverted might emphasize characteristics such as inner quietness and the ability to be, whereas a person who is more extroverted might emphasize characteristics such as enhanced relationships or altruism. There is also some variation in terms of the degree of wakefulness people experience. Obviously, the higher the degree of wakefulness, the more intensely these characteristics will manifest themselves.

In TTT the new self-system of wakefulness unfolds naturally, as if it has been latent inside the shifters, ready to emerge and waiting for the opportunity. It's almost as if this new self-system is latent within the human race collectively, waiting to emerge as the next stage in our development as a species. (I will return to this idea in the final chapter.)

Suicide and Spiritual Awakening

Another interesting aspect that has emerged from my research is the connection between suicide and spiritual awakening. Several of the shifters we've heard from, particularly in chapters 6 and 7, reached a point of seriously contemplating suicide. Some of them (such as Suzy in chapter 4, Donna and Parker in chapter 6, and Nikki in chapter 7) reached the point of planning their own deaths, while Eve — in the last chapter — actually did attempt suicide.[3]

Why is there a connection between suicide and spiritual awakening? As I pointed out in chapter 6, it is because contemplating or attempting suicide denotes a point where the ego has been broken down. All psychological attachments have dissolved away — all the concepts that provide us with a sense of identity and of well-being, such as our hopes, ambitions, and beliefs, our sense of self-esteem, and our sense of status and success. To a large extent, such psychological attachments are the building blocks of the ego, so without them, the ego cracks to pieces. It is also important that a suicidal intention means arriving at a point of surrender and acceptance. It means that we've given up all hope and all effort to change our lives or ourselves. As I have already suggested, an attitude of acceptance (or surrender, or letting go) is often the catalyst of TTT.

At the same time, it's important to point out that spiritual awakening doesn't appear to be a *common* effect of suicide attempts. Most people who attempt suicide go on to make further attempts — in fact, the strongest predictor of suicide is a history of previous attempts. This obviously wouldn't be the case if the person regularly underwent awakening with suicide attempts.

This leads us to the question of why TTT occurs, and why it happens to some people but not others. In the following section, I will offer my explanation of the phenomenon of transformation through turmoil and address some other relevant questions. I've already touched on some of the ideas and issues in passing, but here I'll provide a more concise summary. To make this section easier to digest, I've structured it in a simple question-and-answer format.

Why Does Transformation through Turmoil Occur?

Transformation through turmoil is the result of ego-dissolution, which can occur in two ways. The first is through intense shock, anxiety, stress, or depression, when they create so much psychological tension that psychological structures break down. Usually this happens after many years — even decades — of discord and tension. For example, in chapter 6, we saw how Simon underwent TTT after years of stress and anxiety, while Donna and Parker shifted after many years of depression. But this type of ego-dissolution can also occur with a sudden intense shock, as in the cases of bereavement we looked at in chapter 4. To return to the house analogy, it's as if, in the shock of bereavement, the house of the ego collapses in a sudden violent earthquake, while in other cases (such as with Donna and Parker) it collapses after years of regular minor tremors, which gradually weaken it. For many people, this sudden collapse of the ego may simply equate to a psychotic break, with all the suffering that entails but without any transformative effects. But for a few individuals, it isn't just a breakdown but also a "shift up." A new sense of identity emerges into the vacuum that has been left, like a butterfly emerging from a chrysalis.

The second — and in my research, the most common — way in which ego-dissolution can occur is through the breakdown of psychological attachments. As I noted in relation to suicide above, a psychological attachment is a mental construct that builds up our sense of identity and gives us a sense of security and well-being. Under normal circumstances, we are attached to a lot of mental constructs, such as hopes and ambitions for the future, beliefs about life and the world, our accumulated knowledge, our accomplishments and achievements, our appearance, and so on. At a more tangible level, we may be psychologically attached to possessions, social roles (as spouses or parents or professions), or to other people whose approval and attention we crave. These attachments are the building blocks of our identity. We feel that we are "someone" because of our hopes, beliefs, status, jobs, relationships, possessions, and so on.

However, in times of crisis and turmoil, these psychological attachments break down. In fact, this is usually the root cause of psychological turmoil or depression: we feel lost and desperate because these attachments have been taken away. We have lost the hopes, status, and beliefs (and other attachments) that held together our identity. As a result, we feel empty and fragmented, and full of discord. We are stripped down to nothing, naked and desolate, as if we have been destroyed.

But we are also paradoxically close to transformation. Now that the old ego has dissolved away, there is an empty space within our being. As a result, there is an opportunity for a higher self to emerge into the empty space. All the time, this higher self was latent inside us, fully formed and waiting for the opportunity to awaken. But while the old ego was in place, there was no space for it. But now it's free to rise, like a phoenix from the ashes of the old ego, and to take over as our normal identity.

Let's now go through some of the different types of turmoil we've covered in this book and examine how each brings about a dissolution of the ego. We'll see that this is the main reason why all these different types of turmoil hold so much spiritual potential.

One thing to bear in mind in this discussion is that the two modes of ego-dissolution I've described are difficult to separate and often merge and combine to some degree. It's probably impossible for anyone to go through a breakdown of psychological attachments without experiencing some degree of anxiety and stress. So in most cases, at least to some extent, there are two different processes destabilizing the house of the ego. At the same time as suffering the earthquake tremors of anxiety, stress, and depression, the ego is being gradually dismantled, brick by brick, as psychological attachments break down.

In chapters 2 and 3, we saw that incarceration holds a great deal of spiritual potential, mainly because prisoners are forced to let go of their psychological attachments, resulting in a loss of identity. (Also significant are the inactivity and solitude of prison life, allowing for self-reflection and self-exploration.) In prison, a person leaves behind their social roles, status, achievements, possessions, hopes, and everything else that defines them. All those things lie outside the prison walls. As a result, the ego loses all its reference points and supporting foundations. It dissolves away and — in some cases at least — a new self may emerge from its ashes. (Hence the name of the Prison Phoenix Trust, which provides spiritual support for prisoners in the UK.)

In chapter 4 we saw that bereavement also holds a great deal of spiritual potential. As I noted above, this is probably mainly due to the stress and shock of suddenly losing someone close to us, but the breakdown of psychological attachments is undoubtedly an important factor as well. In bereavement, this happens both directly and indirectly. There is a direct breakdown of attachments in relation to the person who has died — not just to them personally but also to the roles we played in their lives, as a spouse, parent, and so on. And more indirectly, amid the devastation and depression of losing a loved one, many of the things we are attached to — such as our ambitions, beliefs, possessions, and status — may appear so meaningless that we simply let go of them.

The latter point also applies to facing our own death and is one of the reasons why, as we saw in chapter 5, encounters with mortality can lead to spiritual awakening. In a similar way to a bereavement, becoming aware of our own mortality may release us from our psychological attachments. There may be an instantaneous realization that our status, achievements, wealth, and possessions are meaningless. Our future hopes and ambitions appear meaningless because we may not even have a future. Our wealth and possessions become meaningless because they will soon be taken from us. This is why a cancer diagnosis in particular holds a great deal of spiritual potential: it makes some people so intensely aware of the reality and inevitability of death that they let go of their psychological attachments.

To go back to the "military awakenings" discussed in chapter 1, I believe the main reason combat holds a good deal of spiritual potential is that it involves encounters with death. In fact, all the veterans featured in chapter 1 described intense mortality encounters, either through coming close to death themselves or by witnessing the deaths of other people. Gus described his intense fear of death while waiting to go into battle on the Falkland Islands and then how he suddenly become free of that fear in a moment of awakening. David told the story of discovering an Iraqi soldier who was close to death and comforting him during his final moments. At the same time, as with bereavement, it's likely that the sheer anxiety and stress of warfare is a vital part of its association with TTT.

Near-death experiences hold even more spiritual potential than either bereavement or combat. In fact, they probably hold the most spiritual potential of any experience we can undergo. In addition to being encounters with mortality, NDEs almost always include mystical experiences of love, light, and joy, along with out-of-body experiences in which people often meet benevolent spiritual beings or deceased relatives. So the spiritual potential of an IME is intensified by the powerful transformational effects of intense mystical and out-of-body experiences.

Finally, addiction can be seen as a process of the dissolution of psychological attachments. Over long periods of addiction, such as Nikki's or Eve's, people gradually lose everything. They lose their social roles and status, their emotional connections to friends and relatives, their self-respect, their hope and ambitions, and eventually, in most cases, their money and possessions. At the end of this process, they "bottom out," as AA refers to it. They reach a point of being completely lost and broken, when the house of the ego has been completely demolished. And this means that there is now space for a latent higher self to emerge within them.

Why Doesn't TTT Happen to Everyone?

When I give talks about TTT, people often ask why this transformation doesn't happen to everyone. Surely we all go through intense psychological suffering at some point — usually at *many* points — in our lives. We all experience bereavement, for example, while most of us experience intense stress or depression or serious illness. So why aren't we all spiritually awakened?

You could ask the same question about some of the more unusual types of turmoil we've looked at in this book. Since all soldiers are faced with death and experience intense stress and anxiety, why don't we hear about more soldiers undergoing TTT? And why don't we hear about more prisoners or addicts who have become spiritually awakened?

I'm certain that TTT is a lot more common than most people realize. I believe that there are thousands, perhaps even hundreds of thousands, of shifters walking among us who don't understand what has happened to them and haven't told anybody else about it. Without a background in spirituality, they may feel confused, and perhaps — like many of the shifters we've heard from in this book — suspect that they've gone mad.

Nevertheless, as I have pointed out, transformation through turmoil is certainly not the general rule. Most soldiers, prisoners, addicts, and cancer patients do not experience it. Post-traumatic growth is certainly common — as noted earlier, research shows that 47 percent of people experience PTG in response to traumatic events. At the moment we don't have any specific figures about the frequency of TTT (I hope we will at some point). But based on my research, I have no doubt that it is much less common than PTG. (If I had to estimate, I would say that fewer than 1 percent of people experience it, with some variation among different types of turmoil.)

So why is it that intense psychological turmoil and suffering lead to awakening in some people but not in others?

Research into PTG can help us here. It turns out that PTG is associated with certain personality types. In particular, people who have the trait of openness — in that they are curious, creative, and imaginative — are more likely to undergo PTG. And the same applies to TTT. Specifically, people with what might be called a "transliminal" type of mind (to use the term coined by the psychologist Michael Thalbourne) are more likely to experience it. People with a transliminal mind have softer psychological boundaries and are empathic, intuitive, and creative.[4] They are more likely to have spiritual experiences and to experience paranormal phenomena. Essentially, to have a transliminal mind means that your ego is not as solid and rigid as normal, with less of a sense of separation and individuation.

Or to put it differently, we could say that a softer or more labile sense of ego, with thinner boundaries, makes a person more likely to experience TTT. To return to the house analogy, here it's as if the house is made of softer, more pliable materials, such as wood or straw or soil, rather than stone or concrete.

TTT is also dependent on a person's *attitude* to their psychological turmoil. First, it is more likely to occur if a person is prepared to acknowledge the reality of their predicament. Understandably, people may not be prepared to accept the fact that they are an addict or that they are so seriously ill they're in danger of dying. They may be in a state of denial or self-delusion, refusing to contemplate the reality of their predicament and repressing their anxiety and sadness. As a result, it is unlikely that they will experience TTT.

When we face up to the reality of a dangerous predicament, we also face up to our own psychological turmoil. Rather than being estranged from ourselves in delusion and denial, we go *into* our own being, exploring our inner being and our feelings. This kind of self-exploration may also help to bring about TTT. We saw this process in Gus's and David's stories in chapter 1. Both of them began to explore their own being through meditation, and realized how their suffering was created by their thoughts.

In terms of attitude, the most important aspect of TTT is *acceptance*. When we go through challenges and suffering, we often go into a mode of resistance, such as when we talk about fighting a disease or struggling to overcome obstacles. But doing so blocks transformation. When we shift into a mode of acceptance — which can occur in the form of surrendering to a situation, letting go, or handing over our problems — then the transformational potential of suffering is released inside us.

Some shifters can identify the particular moment when their transformation occurred, and this often coincides with a shift into a mode of acceptance. In *Out of the Darkness*, I described how Kevin experienced a sudden shift when, as an alcoholic engaged in the AA recovery process, he "handed over" his problem. In the same book, I told the story of the author Michael Hutchison, who became severely disabled after a fall while he was running. He underwent a shift when he heard a voice inside his head say, "Let go, man, let go. Look at how you're holding on. What do you think life's telling you?"[5]

Among the shifters in this book, in addition to the suicide-related acceptance and surrender just discussed, Ananta experienced transformation when she surrendered to her pain and "dropped into" it. As she said, "It was excruciating, but I had to surrender to it. There was nothing else left to do." Similarly, Amber, whose transformation through addiction we looked at briefly in the last chapter, described how her shift occurred when she "had completely given up the notion that I was in control of anything, really, and was finally honest to myself and to my family about what I really was." In chapter 4 (on bereavement) we also saw how Mirtha made a conscious attempt to acknowledge and explore the mental turmoil she felt after her son's death. As she put it, "In the middle of the turmoil, I was invaded by an inexplicable sense of peace. I knew it was because I had just surrendered. This peace has not left me since then."

One further factor explains why not everyone experiences TTT.

Some people simply seem to be *ready* for the transformation. There appears to be a fully formed, latent higher self inside them, waiting to emerge as soon as the ego dissolves. You could compare it to a bird being ready to hatch as soon as the shell of ego breaks. Perhaps, in other people, this latent higher self isn't fully formed or ready to emerge. So when they experience ego-dissolution, it's simply a painful experience of loss and fragmentation, without the emergence of a new self.

I admit that as yet I have no clear idea why some people seem to be ready for transformation while others don't. If you accept the possibility of reincarnation, then one possibility is that some people are ready for transformation because of spiritual development in their previous lives.

Do Other Factors Make TTT More Likely to Occur?

Meditation definitely facilitates gradual TTT. In chapter 1, Gus's gradual awakening was related to his discovery and practice of Buddhist meditation. In the same chapter, David described how he began to spontaneously meditate while he was a soldier, "paying attention to the breath going in and out, the pattern of breathing.... I had no idea that it was a kind of meditation." In chapters 2 and 3, almost all the shifters who experienced TTT in prison started to practice meditation, leading to a shift some time afterward. Sri Aurobindo began to meditate intensively in prison, as did Ed Little, Adrian, and Ananta. In the case of Sri Aurobindo, Adrian, and Ed (and possibly Ananta too), the shift actually occurred while they were meditating.

Meditation supports the process of acknowledgment, self-exploration, and acceptance described above. When a person meditates, they enter and explore their own being. They face up to their predicament and explore the negative feelings it generates. This may lead to a shift into a mode of acceptance, bringing transformation.

We could also add that inactivity and solitude help to facilitate TTT. This is because inactivity and solitude encourage us to enter into ourselves, so that we face up to our inner turmoil and explore it. As previously mentioned, this is part of the reason for the powerful spiritual potential of imprisonment.

Why Are Some TTT Experiences Disruptive and Not Others?

It's certainly quite common for TTT to be disruptive. Gradual spiritual awakening usually isn't disruptive, because you have the chance to adapt to it and to integrate it into your life. You could compare it to slowly becoming a prominent public figure or celebrity over a long period of time. You have a better chance of remaining stable and sane than if fame suddenly erupts around you, without any preparation or any chance to adjust. In some cases, sudden and dramatic awakenings are fairly smooth too. In this book, we've seen a few examples of people who adapted to their new state quickly and easily — for example, David Ditchfield in chapter 5, Parker in chapter 6, and Eve and Nikki in chapter 7.

On the other hand, we have seen several examples of people who struggled to adapt to their new awakened state, going through long periods of confusion and disruption. This was the case with Ananta and Adrian (in chapter 3), LeeAnn (in chapter 4), and Donna and Simon (in chapter 6). In these cases, TTT disrupts the stable structures of the mind-body organism, throwing everything into disarray. People feel overwhelmed and disoriented, flooded with new information and experience. Now that their ego-boundaries have dissolved away, repressed trauma rises to the surface. They find it hard to function in the everyday world. They struggle to talk to other people and to hold down jobs. They may have problems keeping track of time, or with memory and concentration. Without a framework to understand their transformation, they may — like Adrian or Simon — wonder if they've gone mad. (If you remember,

Adrian wondered if he had caught rabies in Africa and read through the symptoms of psychiatric disorders, without finding any diagnosis that fit his experience.)

Sometimes the disruptive effects of awakening are so severe that they do resemble psychosis. As a result it's unfortunately not uncommon for shifters to be misdiagnosed with psychiatric disorders. They are sometimes prescribed medication (as some of the shifters in this book were) and even committed. However, shifters almost always have a powerful inner knowing that they are undergoing a positive change rather than suffering from some form of disorder. As a result, they are usually wary of psychiatrists and reluctant to take medication.

We've seen that it took some of the shifters years to adjust to their state. For example, Donna in chapter 6 described an integration period of about five years, while Ananta described a three-year period of confusion and disorientation until she had confirmation that she had undergone a spiritual awakening. In chapter 6 I described speaking to Simon two years after his awakening, when his state was beginning to stabilize. It's important to remember that shifters always adjust to their state eventually, even if — in extreme cases — it takes ten years or longer. The disturbance always fades away. After the earthquake of sudden awakening, the ground eventually settles again.

One of the causes of disruptive awakenings (which are sometimes referred to as spiritual crises or spiritual emergencies) is a lack of understanding. As we have seen time and time again in this book, if a person doesn't have a framework to make sense of their transformation, they feel confused. They may even doubt their sanity. They may even resist and repress their new awakened state.

This is partly due to the materialist paradigm of our culture, which tells us that our ordinary awareness is the only valid and sane state through which to perceive the world. Unusual states of consciousness, including wakefulness, are pathologized. Any deviation from our normal sleep state is viewed as a form of insanity, since it conflicts with the consensus view of reality. As a result, there is little understanding of (or support for) people who undergo sudden spiritual awakening.

However, we have also seen that this confusion is always temporary. Shifters always make sense of their transformation eventually. They naturally gravitate toward spiritual books and teachings, and as a result — as with David the soldier, Adrian, Eve, and Nikki — they gain a revelatory sense of self-understanding. They realize that they aren't mad after all, that, as Adrian put it in chapter 3, they haven't lost their marbles but found them!

Another important point is that it's not enough just to have a framework to make sense of your awakening — it has to be the *right* framework. For a person who isn't familiar with the idea of spiritual traditions and practices, in our culture the only obvious alternative to secular materialism is conventional religion. In the last chapter, we saw how Nikki interpreted her transformation in terms of born-again Christianity. Although this gave her some temporary support, helping to reassure her that she wasn't crazy, in the end she reached a point of deep confusion and discord. She came to realize that her wakeful awareness was irreconcilable with the rigid beliefs and practices of conventional Christianity and eventually found a spiritual home within the transreligious spirituality of Eckhart Tolle and others.

Let me make one final point on the question of why some awakenings are disruptive while others aren't. As I mentioned in relation to Parker in chapter 6, when people have a very smooth transformation, this may be because they aren't undergoing a full-fledged awakening but simply uncovering a state of wakefulness that had already arisen but was repressed. Because of the lack of understanding of spirituality in our culture, the repression of spiritual experiences is particularly common in children and adolescents. This may lead to spiritual depression — a sense of inner frustration and discord due to alienation from our spiritual nature.

However, in the same way that shifters always learn to make sense of their transformation, repressed awakenings always manifest themselves eventually. Parker's and Donna's experiences illustrate this very clearly (although Donna didn't have a smooth transformation). They both had spiritual awakenings as teenagers, which they repressed because they couldn't make sense of them. But eventually the awakenings broke through the layers of repression — in Donna's case, twenty-five years after her original awakening, and in Parker's case, around fifteen years later. In the same way that you can't stop a baby from being born, you can't prevent a newly born higher self from emerging and replacing the old ego-self.

And so when layers of repression fall away, it may seem like an awakening, but it's actually just an uncovering. It is therefore less likely to be disruptive.

Is TTT Self-Delusion?

In my time as an academic, I have become familiar with a phenomenon that I call "humbugism." Skepticism is a useful attribute, if it means being careful not to accept claims without evidence or justification. But it's not uncommon for scientists and academics to take skepticism to a cynical level, crying "humbug!" at any findings that suggest positivity or optimism. If anyone has the temerity to suggest that human beings are anything more than selfish biological machines and that life is anything more than a meaningless and purposeless process, they are shot down straightaway. The humbugists take pride in unmasking the illusions that we lesser mortals live by and in reminding us of our gullibility. It doesn't matter what the evidence is — if it points toward meaning or purpose or happiness, then it must be flawed.

In line with this attitude, some academics are skeptical about post-traumatic growth, even though it's such a well-researched phenomenon. Such skeptics suggest that PTG is a self-deceptive strategy that people use to deal with difficult situations such as loss and death by trying to exercise some control over an unpredictable world and to bring some hope into a bleak future. They also suggest that people are trying to find meaning in painful experiences that would otherwise seem a waste of time and energy. In other words, people convince themselves that they have developed in a positive way to bring some value to the experience.

Such skepticism could be applied to TTT too. Perhaps the shifters are deceiving themselves in a similar way. I'm pretty sure that, after reading this far, you don't have these kinds of doubts. But let me make a few points, just in case you ever discuss these topics with a humbugist and need some arguments to defend yourself.

One argument against the idea that shifters are deceiving themselves is that, if this were the case, their changes wouldn't be so deep-rooted. If they were just *thinking themselves* into a transformation, then they wouldn't experience such major changes in terms of relationships, interests, attitude, and behavior. It's also very doubtful that these changes would have maintained themselves for so long. As I noted at the beginning of the book, the difference between TTT and born-again religious experiences is that the latter don't tend to hold. However, TTT is almost always permanent. Once the old ego dies, it normally disappears forever. This is why, although some of the shifts we've investigated are fairly recent (for example, Parker's occurred just six months before I interviewed him), others happened a long time ago. Renee's (in chapter 4) happened more than a half century ago, when she was fourteen. Ananta's happened twenty-three years ago, while David Ditchfield's occurred fourteen years before he spoke to me.

A second argument is that self-deception implies regression and impairment. People who deceive themselves evade reality. They become more closed down to their experience and usually don't function well in the world. The self-deception impairs their personality, their mental health, and their relationships. But it's clear that the shifters in this book have experienced an enormous progression, a shift up to a higher mode of functioning across every area of their being and their lives. They have become more altruistic and compassionate, more trusting and accepting, with enhanced well-being, a decreased fear of death, more authentic relationships, a greater sense of connection to nature, and so on. In complete contrast to self-deceptive people, their transformation is all about engaging *more intensely* with reality and becoming more open to their experience.

A third argument is that many of the shifters' relatives and friends recognized that they had undergone major changes. Some of the shifters I interviewed described feeling that they were different people living in the same body, and some of their friends and relatives had the same feeling about them. For example, David Ditchfield's mother told him, "We know that something's happened to you. Since the accident you're just glowing." After his stress-induced transformation (described in chapter 6), two of Simon's children said to him, "Daddy — you've changed. Something's happened." The unfortunate aspect of this is that, in some cases, the shifters' relationships break down. For example, Adrian (in chapter 3) told me that a lot of people had fallen out of his life since his shift, although many new people had come into it too. As we saw in chapter 6, Simon's relationship with his wife broke down. And arguably, only an authentic, deep-rooted transformation — rather than a pretense based on self-deception — would have this kind of impact on other people.

Finally, the fact that some of the shifters went through difficult awakenings, with a lot of confusion and disturbance, makes it unlikely that they were deceiving themselves. If people wanted to give meaning to difficult experiences and make their predicament seem more positive, why would they experience such painful states of disorientation and disturbance? That would be like longing for a luxury vacation to escape from stress and instead choosing to spend two weeks working in a factory.

Is Wakefulness the Same as Enlightenment?

In an effort to understand his remarkable transformation, Simon visited a Buddhist monastery and spoke to one of the chief monks. After hearing his story, the monk said jokingly, "Don't talk too loud about all this — there are a lot of monks here who are trying to attain this state."

Joking apart, this is a meaningful question. So far in this book, we haven't spoken much about spirituality in a traditional sense. I've described a remarkable transformation that some people go through in response to intense suffering. In the majority of cases, the people we have heard from knew little or nothing about spirituality at the time of their transformation. However, almost all of them gravitated toward spiritual teachings and ideas afterward in an attempt to make sense of their experiences. They intuitively knew that the experiences they had were explicable in the context of spirituality.

This leads to the question: Is the state that these shifters experienced the same as the enlightenment that Buddhists speak of or the *samadhi* that Hindu spiritual teachers speak of?

Every spiritual or mystical tradition conceives of an ideal state of being in which people transcend the limitations of normal awareness and wake up to a wider and more intense reality. In this state, we attain fulfillment and contentment and become free of suffering. In most traditions this is described in terms of transcending separateness and achieving union with ultimate reality. In Taoism this state is called *ming*, while in Sufism it is *baqa* (literally, "abiding in God"). In the mystical traditions of Christianity, it is referred to as theosis or deification (that is, becoming one with God), while in mystical Judaism, it is referred to as *devekut* (literally, "cleaving to the divine").

Some scholars of religion emphasize the differences between these concepts and dispute that they are interrelated. And it's true that there are some differences between them. What Buddhists conceive as enlightenment (or *bodhi)* is not quite the same as what Hindus see as *sahaja samadhi* or what Taoists call *ming.* For example, in *samadhi* there is a very strong emphasis on union with the universe (which is, after all, the literal meaning of *yoga)*, while the Buddhist concept of enlightenment does not emphasize union so much as self-sufficiency and transcending the illusion of separateness.

However, I think it's clear that there is a common core in all these concepts.

An apt analogy here would be people looking at a landscape from different vantage points — there will always be slight differences in the way they describe the landscape, even though it's the same one. We should think in terms of a landscape of spiritual experience that followers of different spiritual traditions observe and explore in a slightly different way. They have a different approach and a different viewpoint, determined by their culture and their religious and philosophical traditions. So obviously they will emphasize certain aspects of spiritual experience over others. Nevertheless, it is the *same landscape* they are describing and exploring.

This applies to the shifters too. They are exploring the same landscape of expansive human experience that spiritual traditions refer to. For them, the only difference is that they have stumbled into this landscape *accidentally*, in reaction to intense suffering. In contrast, the adherents of spiritual traditions explore the landscape more consciously and systematically, through spiritual practices like meditation and lifestyle guidelines that are designed to cultivate wakefulness. You could say that the shifters have landed in this landscape through a dramatic fall, as if they have parachuted into it from a plane. On the other hand, spiritual seekers follow paths that have been marked by previous seekers and their traditions. This explains why spiritual seekers don't experience the same degree of disruption and difficulty that shifters often undergo after awakening. As I mentioned before in relation to gradual cases of TTT, the gradual approach of adherents to traditions gives them time to get used to the landscape of wakefulness and adjust to its rarified climate. In contrast, shifters may initially find the landscape strange and overwhelming.

My feeling is that, because the shifters' experiences occur outside spiritual traditions, they are especially valuable. They reveal the wakeful state to us in a more naked state, free from the conceptions and interpretations that are often superimposed by spiritual traditions. I certainly don't want to denigrate spiritual traditions, since I have a deep respect for them. I feel great reverence for Hindu and Buddhist traditions in particular, which have enriched my life greatly. But we need to remember that wakefulness in its essence transcends all spiritual traditions. Wakefulness is an experiential state that exists in itself, before being interpreted in various ways by different traditions.

It is therefore possible to go beyond traditions and explore wakefulness in a more essential form. (Indeed, that is what I have been trying to do throughout this book.) Of course, there's really no such thing as *pure* experience. People will always interpret and describe experiences in different ways according to their language, culture, and personalities. But there are differing layers of interpretation, and when we look at wakefulness outside spiritual traditions, I think we are removing some layers and getting closer to the essence of experience.

In other words, I am sure that the Buddhist monk Simon spoke to is correct. The shifters are indeed experiencing the ideal state that all spiritual and mystical traditions aspire to.

One final question is so vital that I will devote the whole of the next chapter to it: What can we learn from the shifters' transformations and integrate into our own paths of spiritual development?

9

LEARNING FROM TRANSFORMATION THROUGH TURMOIL

W̱e can learn from the shifters and their transformational experiences in two main ways. First, they can teach us how to respond to suffering and turmoil when these arise in our lives. Second, the psychological processes of their transformations offer us some basic principles that we can apply as practices and guidelines in our own spiritual development.

I have already developed some methods and techniques based on what I've learned from the shifters, which I regularly use in workshops and online courses. I will describe some of these techniques below. (I also describe many of them in my *Return to Harmony* audio course, which I recommend if you would like further detail and closer guidance.)

Part One: Harnessing the Transformational Power of Suffering

We don't have a choice about whether suffering arises in our lives. As the Buddha pointed out, suffering is a part of human life. No matter how safe and secure we make our life situations, adversity always breaks in. No matter how much we may try to avoid them, tragic events like bereavement, disease, and death inevitably afflict us at some point.

What we do have a choice about is how to *respond* to suffering. This was one of the insights that the psychologist Viktor Frankl gained during his three years as an inmate of Nazi concentration camps. Frankl was one of the 10 percent of inmates who survived Auschwitz, and as we saw in chapter 2, he attributed his survival to his strong sense of purpose. He watched other inmates give up hope, losing their ideals and sense of purpose, and noticed that soon afterward they would succumb to illness and death. As he wrote in his famous book about his wartime experiences, *Man's Search for Meaning*, "Everything can be taken from a man but one thing: the last of the human freedoms — to choose one's attitude in any given set of circumstances, to choose one's own way."[1]

In this book, we've looked at types of suffering and turmoil that have a high degree of transformational potential, but *all* types of suffering and turmoil have some degree of this potential. Deep inside the darkest moments of our lives lies a golden core of spiritual power, which can wake us up and transform our identity and our lives.

In fact, simply to be *aware* that suffering can have some positive effects may be beneficial. This knowledge may bring us greater courage and resilience when we face suffering. It means that we don't have to see suffering as a terrifying enemy to shrink away from. I don't mean that we should welcome suffering or purposely seek it out. But when it does arise in our lives — as it inevitably will — we should remind ourselves that we may gain something from it. Suffering may be our greatest teacher rather than our greatest enemy. Even more than that, it can be our guru, a catalyst for spiritual transformation.

So how do we gain access to this golden core hidden within our suffering?

A Four-Step Process of Responding to Challenges

In the last chapter we saw that TTT is facilitated by an attitude of acknowledgment and acceptance, along with self-exploration. Based on this, I have developed a four-step process of responding to suffering and turmoil to help us harness their transformational power.

Step 1: Acknowledge Your Predicament

When you face turmoil or tragedy, you will probably feel the "avoidance impulse." This impulse is natural — it's the same impulse that makes us shrink from pain or run away from danger. You might feel the urge to numb yourself to the reality of your predicament and to your inner turmoil by drinking or taking drugs (including prescribed medication) or by obsessively immersing yourself in distractions like TV, socializing, or work.

But although it may seem to help initially, avoidance is self-defeating. If we avoid negative feelings, they build up on a subconscious level, eventually becoming so intense that they burst through our defenses. Avoidance also denies us access to the transformational potential of psychological turmoil.

If you have been diagnosed with cancer, it's understandable that you might find it hard to face up to the fact that your life is in danger, and that you may only have a limited time left. If you suffer a bereavement, you might find it hard to accept the reality of your loss and the fact you will never see your loved one again. But it's vital that you find the courage to acknowledge the reality of your predicament rather than distracting yourself from it. Find a quiet moment when you're alone (or with a therapist or supportive partner) and inactive, without any distractions. Turn your attention toward your predicament and allow yourself to contemplate it. Contemplate how your circumstances have changed, and what the future might hold for you.

This will be uncomfortable at first, of course. But you'll probably find that it isn't as painful as you expected. You'll soon discover new courage and resilience inside you and realize that you've underestimated your coping abilities.

Step 2: Acknowledge Your Negative Thoughts and Feelings

Once you've faced up to the reality of your predicament, the next stage is to face up to your inner turmoil — your feelings of anxiety, anger, and pain.

Here we can make a good analogy with physical pain. Although our natural impulse is to recoil from pain, sometimes it's more beneficial to move toward it. Let me illustrate this with an example from my life. My wife suffers from migraines, and for years now we have practiced an exercise in which I encourage her to move toward the pain rather than shrink away from it. I guide her toward the source of the pain until her attention merges with it. I tell her: "As you merge with it, the pain no longer feels sharp and concentrated. It begins to dissipate and to spread through your being, becoming softer and weaker, like salt dissolving in water. You feel that you're one with it, that it's a part of your being. And now it's no longer a pain but a sensation. It feels numb, a soft throbbing sensation, that even feels welcoming and pleasant."

You can follow a similar process with psychological or emotional pain. The avoidance impulse will try to pull you away from your inner being, into distraction and activity. But again, in a time of quietness, turn your attention to your inner subjective world.

First, observe your thoughts. What kind of negative thoughts are flowing through your mind? Verbalize them. You may find it helpful to write them down.

Then move toward your negative feelings. Acknowledge your inner turmoil and pain. Don't be ashamed of it — accept it as an inevitable response to your predicament, in the same way that physical pain is an inevitable response to an injury.

Again, in the acknowledgment of your inner pain, you will feel strong. You will sense a deep resilience inside you, enabling you to cope with the pain. You will find that the pain isn't as acute as you feared.

Step 3: Explore Your Inner Being

Once you've acknowledged your negative thoughts and feelings, the next step is to *explore* them and how they're affecting you. What is the source of the pain inside you? Is it located in a particular part of your being or body? What feelings are you experiencing — grief, anger, anxiety, loss? Which feeling is hurting you most?

As you acknowledge and explore your thoughts and feelings, be aware of the distinction between you and them. Be aware that you are not your thoughts and feelings. You are an observer, watching your thoughts and feelings like a person watching a film on a screen. Try to anchor yourself in your identity as the observer, being aware . of the space between you and your thoughts and feelings.

As discussed in my book *The Leap*, Graham described to me the tragedy of the deaths of both his wife and his teenage son: "Almost overnight I had lost two important roles in my life: I had been a husband for twenty years and a father for seventeen years. The sense of who I was had been stripped away, and I was left staring at emptiness." However, as a Buddhist, Graham was used to entering his mental space and observing his thoughts and feelings. Here he beautifully describes this process of acknowledging and exploring his own inner turmoil:

> There were tears of pain, of course, but I knew that if I turned towards the feelings of emptiness and despair and explored them, rather than resisting them, I would be able to move on. Within the emptiness there was stillness that somehow reassured me that 'all was well.' These events pulled me up short. It was a trigger, stopping me in my tracks, forcing me to take stock of my life. I was no longer a husband, no longer a father, I haven't got a job. What does it mean?[2]

Step 4: Accept Your Predicament and Your Turmoil

The final stage is to accept both your predicament and your inner turmoil. In a sense, all three of the previous stages are part of the process of acceptance, so you could think of this fourth stage simply as the culmination of the process.

When we resist our predicaments, we oppose reality with our thoughts. This causes conflict with the world and creates discord inside us. Acceptance means dropping our opposition to reality and falling into harmony with the world. It means surrendering to what is rather than wishing for an alternate reality. Whereas resistance creates duality between us and reality, acceptance creates oneness.

It's important to remember that, as the above summary suggests, acceptance is not something that we actively *do*. You don't make an effort to accept a situation; rather, you *let go* of the effort to resist it. You don't change anything but simply let go of the *desire* to change the situation. That's why acceptance feels so liberating — because it means releasing tension and relaxing rather than fighting reality.

So now let me guide you through a process of letting go of resistance to any situation. I want you to imagine that there is a cord connecting you to your predicament, stretched so tight that it's causing tension. Now imagine that the cord is gently dissolving away, evaporating, releasing your resistance and your tension. As you imagine the cord dissolving, allow yourself to open up to your predicament, embracing the reality of your life.

If you find this tricky, it may help to align the process with your breathing. Take a deep breath in, and as you breathe out, imagine that you are releasing your resistance. Imagine that the cord that connects you to your predicament is dissolving. As you release your resistance, feel yourself accepting and embracing reality. You can also try saying out loud to yourself as you breathe out, "I release my resistance." You can repeat this as many times as you like, until you feel that your resistance has faded away and that you have become one with the predicament, and with your life as it is.

As a final part of this process, imagine that the whole of your life is spread out before you, as a panoramic landscape — including every activity and task that your life involves, every aspect of your life situation, and every aspect of life itself, such as aging and death. As you survey the landscape, accept it all, exactly as it is. Imagine stretching your arms out wide, embracing every aspect of your life.

By this point, you will hopefully feel a sense of liberation and lightness, now that you're no longer carrying the burden of your resistance. You may feel a sense of inner harmony, now that you're no longer fighting against reality and no longer filled with the inner tension of your resistance.

Even more, by now you will hopefully sense the transformational power of suffering. You may sense that you have somehow opened up inside, gained access to deep levels of your being, and uncovered new reserves of resilience and well-being. You may even feel that, in your moment of acceptance, the old ego self that was mounting the resistance against your predicament has dissolved away. And out of its ashes, a glorious new self has arisen and taken its place.

Part Two: Applying TTT to Our Own Spiritual Development

Let's turn now to the second way in which we can learn from the shifters, applying the principles of their transformational experiences to our own lives. I'm going to suggest three ways in which we can do this: embracing challenge, consciously detaching, and contemplating death. I will go through these in turn.

Embracing Challenge

There's one extreme and simplistic way in which we can apply the shifters' experiences: by consciously inflicting suffering on ourselves. Since we know that such situations can be transformational, why shouldn't we make a conscious effort to become addicts or prisoners or soldiers? Or perhaps — on a less absurd level — we could follow the lead of religious ascetics by avoiding pleasure and comfort and inflicting physical pain on ourselves.

These methods would obviously be far too dangerous, both physically and mentally. And there's no guarantee that they would work. It is doubtful that TTT can be consciously replicated, since part of the transformational power of traumatic experiences comes from their sudden and unexpected occurrence. So it may not be possible for us to stage them.

Nevertheless, I think we can take one general lesson from the shifters: we should embrace challenges, even if they involve hardship and sacrifice. When we avoid challenges and our lives become easy and stable, we are more likely to fall asleep. We may lose touch with our deep reserves of resilience, creativity, and skill and live well below our potential. Challenge and effort can reawaken us and lift us up to a higher functioning level.

In fact, many people realize this instinctively and make a habit of putting themselves into difficult and even dangerous situations as a way of waking themselves up. This is part of the reason why people climb mountains or run marathons, or practice extreme sports such as paragliding or bungee jumping. People sense that challenges such as these are character building, leading to increased confidence and resilience. You could even say that this is a kind of voluntary post-traumatic growth — that is, people choose to put themselves in difficult and even traumatic situations as a way of harnessing their developmental potential. They know intuitively that by surmounting the challenges, they will gain some of the same benefits that people gain accidentally after traumatic incidents — that they will become more confident and competent, more appreciative of their lives, and so on. In extreme cases, it is possible that people are enacting a subconscious impulse to expose themselves to the danger of dying in order to gain some of the psychological benefits of encountering death, such as greater appreciation and a new sense of purpose or meaning.

In addition, I think that people practice such activities because of their consciousness-changing effect. Demanding and challenging activities are effective ways of inducing states of flow (or intense absorption), and even awakening experiences. They provide a powerful focus for our attention, which quiets our minds and brings us into a state of complete presence.

This is also why many of us like to challenge ourselves in a more general way, by uprooting ourselves from comfortable situations such as steady jobs and relationships or familiar home environments. Part of us enjoys stability and comfort, but another part pulls us away from them. That part of us hungers for growth and so rebels against safety and security, encouraging us to seek new challenges and environments.

So without recommending extremes of self-denial or danger, I would suggest following an adventurous lifestyle in which we embrace challenges because of their potential for development and awakening. In other words, I would encourage you to practice voluntary post-traumatic growth.

Consciously Detaching

A more significant lesson we can learn from the shifters is to live in a mode of *detachment*. By this I don't mean a state of emotional detachment, in which we are indifferent to other people or world affairs. I mean a state in which we don't derive our identity and well-being from external things or mental concepts; I mean a state of being inwardly content and self-sufficient without attachment to possessions, achievements, roles, status, and ambitions.

As we saw in the last chapter, in psychological terms the dissolution of attachments is the most important aspect of the shifters' transformations. Since attachments are the building blocks of the ego, the dissolution of attachments leads to the dissolution of the ego itself, which allows a latent higher self to be born.

In this section I will show you how to practice a conscious form of detachment.

Becoming Aware of Your Attachments

First, we need to become aware of our attachments. Sometimes we have carried attachments for so long, and they have attached themselves to us so subtly, that we may not even be conscious of them.

There are so many different types of attachments that it's difficult to describe them all. In their most obvious and "heaviest" form, attachments occur in the form of addiction — physical addiction to substances like drugs, cigarettes, food, or chocolate, and psychological addiction to electronic devices or to social media. Slightly less overtly, we may be attached to material objects, such as money and possessions. We may also be attached to our own bodies as material objects, caring excessively about our appearance or feeling depressed about the process of aging.

Less overtly still but perhaps most significant of all are our conceptual attachments. For example, we might be attached to our conceptual identity as a member of a national or ethnic group or to our identity and role as a spouse, parent, sibling, and so on. We might be attached to a concept of our status or achievements, feeling that we are "important" and successful people, superior to others. We may be attached in a similar way to our beliefs, our hopes, and our ambitions.

All these attachments build our sense of identity and hold together our ego as a structure. As already suggested, you can picture them as the building blocks of the ego.

In my workshops I often give people a list of different types of attachments and ask them to consider how attached they are to each one. Awareness is liberating in itself. To an extent, simply being aware of your attachments helps you to become free of them.

At the same time, we can take steps to free ourselves from attachments, which I will guide you through now.

Detaching through Spiritual Practice

One of the best ways to help free ourselves from attachments is simply to practice meditation or to follow a spiritual path of some form. Fundamentally, we need attachments because of our separate and fragile ego. Our attachments bolster and reinforce the ego so that it no long feels so vulnerable. So the most fundamental way of releasing ourselves from attachments is to heal the ego itself. This means cultivating a state of inner well-being and wholeness, which removes the need to seek identity and well-being outside ourselves. Without a sense of ego-separation, we won't feel a sense of lack and fragility, so we will be able to let go of our attachments.

This is the main aim of meditation: to soften the ego as a structure so that its boundaries become weaker and we transcend our normal sense of separation. Meditation helps us to feel connected rather than separate, as if we were participating rather than just observing, without a sense of lack or fragility. It's as if a broken fragment has become part of the whole again.

This is both a long- and short-term effect of meditation. If you had a good meditation this morning, you probably experienced the sense of connection and inner wholeness I've just described. Perhaps it lingered for an hour or two afterward, or perhaps longer — perhaps it's still inside you now. However, it usually fades away once we have returned to our busy everyday lives and needs to be rekindled by another meditation practice later, or the following day.

At the same time, over the years or decades that you have practiced meditation, an *ongoing* sense of wholeness has been building up inside you. Even though you may still experience a more intense sense of wholeness when you meditate, the baseline of your normal state has changed. Over the years, your ego boundaries have become softer; your sense of self has become less fragile and separate. As a result — even though you may not be consciously aware of it, since the change has been gradual — your need for psychological attachments has diminished, and you have become less attached to external sources of identity and well-being.

Every spiritual path is a movement beyond ego-separateness and toward connection and union. This is part of the reason why most spiritual traditions emphasize cultivating compassion and practicing acts of service and kindness. By serving others, we transcend our own self-centered desires and ambitions and so move beyond ego-separateness. In this sense, practicing service and altruism can also indirectly help to dissolve our psychological attachments.

Most spiritual traditions also advocate detachment more explicitly. They emphasize a life of simplicity and moderation, without attachment to sensory pleasures or unnecessary possessions. They encourage us to be content with our present life situation rather than being attached to ambitions. They encourage us to be humble rather than to be attached to notions of status and achievement.

Any path or practice that helps you to cultivate inner well-being and wholeness will reduce your need for psychological attachments. You won't need attachments anymore in the same way that a completed building doesn't need scaffolding or support.

Breaking Attachments

There are also more direct ways we can use to liberate ourselves from psychological attachments. While following spiritual practices, we can simply make a conscious effort to weaken our attachments. This might sound challenging, but it's important to remember that, although our psychological attachments may have *originated* in response to psychological need, in some cases (particularly if you have already begun to meditate or to follow a spiritual practice) they continue as *habits*. In other words, the attachments may remain intact even if we no longer have a psychological need for them, simply as habit patterns. This makes it fairly easy for us to free ourselves from them.

And even if this is not the case — that is, even if there is still some degree of psychological need — you might be surprised at how quickly you can adjust to the absence of the attachment. After an initial sense of loss and insecurity, you'll quickly grow stronger. Your essential self will grow into the space left by the attachment, bringing a greater sense of wholeness.

I experienced this many years ago when I gave up smoking. After smoking heavily (twenty-five to thirty roll-up cigarettes a day) for twelve years, I decided to stop on my thirtieth birthday. I had heard many stories about the difficulties of giving up smoking, but for me — once I'd covered the physical withdrawal symptoms by chewing nicotine gum — it wasn't such an ordeal. After about three weeks of conscious effort (which in itself was not particularly arduous), I was surprised to find that the urge to smoke quickly died away. But what I found even more surprising was the feeling of new strength and wholeness that filled me. It was as if the part of myself that I had sacrificed to my addiction had been given back to me in a natural process of adjustment and healing. I'm sure that this was because, over the previous year or so, I had undergone significant psychological healing. I had started meditating regularly and become a vegetarian. I had also met my future wife. As a result, I probably no longer had a strong psychological need to smoke. My sense of self was more connected and whole, and so I didn't need the support of cigarettes anymore. To a large extent, I only had the habit to deal with rather than the psychological need. If there *was* still some psychological need, it evaporated in the process of giving up the attachment.

I would recommend making a similar attempt to weaken your attachments. For example, you might try to weaken your attachment to money and possessions by refraining from buying unnecessary things and following a simpler, more frugal lifestyle. You might try to weaken your attachment to your appearance by no longer wearing fashionable clothes or dyeing your hair. You may try to weaken your attachment to status and attention by making a conscious effort to stop obsessively posting on social media and incessantly trying to increase your number of followers.

This might feel uncomfortable at first but — particularly if you're already following a spiritual practice — you'll quickly begin to feel a new sense of inner strength and wholeness. Even if there is still some degree of psychological need for the attachment, a process of inner healing will take place, and your essential self will grow into the space left by the attachment, filling you with a sense of new strength and wholeness.

I would also like to recommend a specific meditation practice to help dissolve your psychological attachments. In my *Return to Harmony* audio course, I guide listeners through a twenty-minute detachment meditation. I don't have space to describe the full meditation, but here I'll offer a summary.

The meditation consists of contemplating different types of psychological attachments one by one and letting go of them, similar to the acceptance exercise described above. We contemplate each attachment, reminding ourselves of how unnecessary it is and why it can't bring us true fulfillment. Then we make a mental intention to release each attachment.

We begin this process with possessions and money, then focus on conceptual attachments such as beliefs, ambitions, and achievement or status. Then we let go of attachment to our appearance, and then to the concept of age, and then to our names. We remind ourselves that the essence of our being has no name, just as it has no age and no physical form. I end the meditation by asking: "So what's left at the end of this process, after we've let go of all our attachments? What's left is the pure essence of our being, which has natural qualities of wholeness and well-being. We can feel those qualities inside us right now. And as we feel them, we know that there is no need for us to depend on anything external. There is no need for us to attach ourselves to anything outside ourselves in search of well-being or identity.

"So now let's rest within the essence of our being, in a state of pure detachment and a state of pure well-being."

Contemplating Death

The third way that we can apply the shifters' experiences to our own spiritual development is by contemplating the reality and inevitability of death. This has been one of the main themes of this book: that encounters with death — whether they occur in the form of IMEs or NDEs — can lead to spiritual awakening. This links to the topic of detachment, because one of the main reasons why encounters with death lead to awakening is that they dissolve away our psychological attachments.

As with TTT in general, it would be absurdly dangerous and irrational for us to actually *stage* encounters with death for their transformational effect (although as I mentioned above, I think that some people do this indirectly and unconsciously when they practice extreme sports and other dangerous activities). Nevertheless, I believe it is possible for us to attain a similar awakening effect simply by seriously and regularly *contemplating* death.

This is another practice used by adherents to some spiritual traditions. In particular, death awareness is strongly emphasized in Buddhism. The Buddha advised his monks to meditate in cemeteries or to sit down next to any dead or decaying bodies they found on their travels. The monks would contemplate the fact that the same fate was awaiting them, that death is real and inevitable, and that life is temporary and fragile. As a result, they would become aware of the impermanence of life and the foolishness of attachment to the world. In the Satipatthana Sutta, the Buddha tells his monks that if they see a dead body — one that is newly dead, one being eaten by animals, or one that is nothing more than a skeleton or a pile of bones — they should tell themselves: "Verily, also my own body is of the same nature; such it will become and will not escape it." In this way, the monk becomes aware of the impermanence of life and, in the Buddhas' words, "lives detached, and clings to nothing in the world."

Many other spiritual teachers have recognized the importance of being aware of death. The early-twentieth-century Russian teacher George Gurdjieff stated that the best way to awaken human beings from sleep would be for everyone to be told the precise date of their death. The Irish spiritual poet John O'Donohue used to run workshops in which he would take participants to the Cliffs of Moher, close to his home on the west coast of Ireland. The cliffs are famous because of their enormous sheer drop. O'Donohue would ask people to lie down with their heads over the edge of the cliffs, gazing at the vast distance between them and the sea below, to make them aware of the reality of death and the precious miracle of life.

In some ways, it seems strange that we need to be reminded of death. After all, we all *know* that we're going to die at some point. But knowledge is not the same as awareness. For many of us, death is not a reality. As we go about our daily lives, we rarely contemplate it. This is partly because, in secular cultures such as those of Europe and the United States, death is a taboo subject. Whereas our ancestors would regularly watch people die and see dead bodies, we're shielded from death by modern medical practices. People usually die in hospitals rather than at home. Soon after death, their bodies are taken to funeral homes, where we usually have to make an appointment to see them.

In addition, many people don't want to talk or think about death, because it makes them feel uneasy. If you don't believe in any form of life after death, then understandably the idea that one day you will disappear off the face of the earth — and suddenly be taken away from everything and everyone you know — may not be a comfortable prospect. To become comfortable with the idea of death entails a good deal of contemplation and preparation. It arises from a long process of acknowledgment and acceptance, which our culture does little to support.

But in my view, there is another, perhaps more fundamental factor in human beings' lack of awareness of death. It's almost as if there is a psychological mechanism that switches off our awareness of death. In previous books (such as *Waking from Sleep*) I have suggested that there is a "desensitizing mechanism" that switches off our attention to familiar experiences. For example, once a place (such as our own neighborhood) has become familiar to us, we stop paying attention to it. We no longer notice colors and detail, or even beautiful landscapes. Phenomena that used to seem strikingly beautiful to us end up appearing mundane — so mundane that we stop paying attention to them.

The same is true for life in general. Life becomes so familiar to us that we take it for granted. The prospect of death becomes unreal, and we unconsciously assume we are immortal. It's almost as if we've been hypnotized and go through life in a kind of trance.

Sometimes, however, when we have an encounter with death — through an accident or illness — we wake up out of this trance. And then, as Mark Nepo told us at the beginning of chapter 5, the world becomes a completely different place.

So how can we make ourselves aware of the reality of death without actually encountering it directly?

I would highly recommend making time every day to contemplate the reality and inevitability of death. Contemplate your own body and how it has changed over the past ten or twenty years. Remember that your existence depends on a vast array of complex biological processes, all working together to keep you alive and conscious from moment to moment. Sooner or later these processes will begin to fail. And they could fail at any moment. No matter how much you try to stay healthy, no matter how much medical treatment you receive, at some point one or more of these processes will break down irreparably and you will die.

It's possible that these processes will break down before you reach old age, due to a sudden accident or an unexpected physical malfunction. In light of this, to be alive in this world and in this form is miraculously fortunate. It's also a temporary and fragile process. It's as if we're on a beautiful vacation but don't know how long it's going to last. All we know is that it's going to end at some point, and that point could occur at any moment. (Note: if contemplating death makes you feel uncomfortable and triggers the avoidance impulse, you should first practice acceptance of death, using the process I outlined earlier in this chapter.)

It may not be feasible for us to meditate next to dead bodies, like Buddhist monks, but we can easily follow a variation of this practice. I recommend regularly visiting your local cemetery, spending some time walking among the gravestones, reading the inscriptions, and contemplating the fact that it is just a matter of time until you will also be dead. Sit on a bench in the cemetery, and as the Buddha suggested, contemplate the fragility and impermanence of life.

In addition, when people close to us are in the process of dying, we should spend time with them. As well as bringing comfort to them, sharing their company will intensify our own awareness of death, as we watch them preparing to take a journey that we will also be making at some point. And when our friends and relatives do die, we should acknowledge and accept the full enormity of the event — including our own sense of loss — without avoidance. As well as helping to harness the transformational effects of bereavement, this will increase awareness of our own mortality.

One specific exercise of contemplating death that I have found very effective is a variation of the Year to Live therapy developed by the poet and author Stephen Levine. In Levine's original guidelines, we imagine that we're going to die exactly one year from now. We treat the next 365 days as if they genuinely are the last days of our life. During the first part of the year, Levine suggests, we should discuss our attitude to death, including our fear of it. Then we should start to review our life, developing an attitude of gratitude for and forgiveness toward people we've known. Later, we should begin to contemplate what will happen to our body after death, then write a will and an epitaph, along with letters and poems for the loved ones we are leaving behind. In the tenth month of the program, we imagine how our possessions are going to be distributed when we die and consciously let go of them. In the eleventh month, we spend more time with relatives and friends, contemplating their mortality too. And finally, in the twelfth month, we say goodbye to our loved ones, thank our body for its perseverance, and prepare for death.

I have used an abbreviated form of this exercise with many groups of students and workshop participants over the years. In my adaptation, I display the date exactly a year from now on a screen. I tell the students that this is the date of their death. They are given a worksheet and asked to contemplate — and write down — what changes they are going to make over the last 365 days of their lives, under different categories such as changes to relationships, lifestyle, and attitude. Then I ask them to stand up and walk around the room, sharing their ideas with the other students. Typically, they say that they will spend more time with their family and friends, spend more time in nature, travel to a place they've always wanted to visit, or take up a hobby they've always wanted to do.

Finally, I tell the students that, although we can't be sure, there is a very strong probability that they are *not* going to die a year from now. Nevertheless, they should still live as if this is the case and carry through with all the intentions they've written down. (At least the ones that aren't impractical. I wouldn't advise them to give up college to go traveling around the world!) And most important of all, they should continue to contemplate death, retaining the awareness that life is short and precious and death is always close at hand.

Almost without fail, this exercise has a powerful positive effect. My students sometimes tell me that it's the first time they have seriously thought about death. Now that death is a reality, they feel a new sense of gratitude for life and an expanded perspective. Temporarily, at least, they awaken from the trance of taking life and the world for granted.

The same is true of any period of contemplation of our own mortality. Death is a perfect representative of suffering as a whole: although we may initially feel anxious about it and have an impulse to shrink away from it, when we seriously contemplate death — or actually encounter it — we find that it has a transformational effect.

By following the above guidelines, you probably won't experience the sudden and dramatic awakenings that the shifters experienced. You probably won't experience the sudden death of your ego and the dramatic birth of a new identity. But you will undergo gradual spiritual development. You will gradually free yourself from the tyranny of the ego-self, allowing your latent and essential awakened self to arise. Eventually your latent awakened self may supplant the old ego entirely. And this will be your own extraordinary awakening.

CONCLUSION

The Most Extraordinary Awakening

One of my favorite artists is the Belgian singer-songwriter Jacques Brel. As well as being an amazing singer and performer, Brel was a great poet who captured a huge variety of human experiences in his songs. The songs are filled with an amazing array of characters, facing all kinds of challenges and hardships: an abandoned lover who goes mad with longing, a dying man saying goodbye to his unfaithful wife, an alcoholic who has drunk his whole life away, a frightened young soldier waiting to lose his virginity in an army-run brothel. Brel's songs and performances have so much intensity that time seems to stop as you listen. Sometimes, at the end of a song, the world seems like a different place.

One of my favorite songs by Brel is "Les Désespérés" (The Desperate Ones). In this beautiful piano ballad, Brel sings about all the desperate people in the world who feel lost, isolated, and unloved. All they know of love is the word *love*. They contemplate suicide, staring at the sweet, deep water under a bridge, which seems to beckon them to the end of their world. At the end of the song, the desperate ones simply disappear into silence, forgotten, as if they had never existed.

I find it moving to listen to the song and contemplate the millions of people all over the world who are living in turmoil and despair — all the millions of people who are desperately lonely or frustrated or depressed, who are seriously ill or oppressed or imprisoned or suffering from addiction. However, after my years of research, I know that some of these desperate people will experience transformation through turmoil. Because they have reached the depths of despair, there is a chance that they will rise to the highest peaks of human well-being.

This applies to all the human beings who have undergone terrible hardship and suffering in the past. As I've mentioned earlier, I find it comforting to think that, out of all the millions of soldiers, prisoners, and bereaved people who have undergone so much suffering and trauma throughout human history, a certain portion of them have undergone awakening. And of course, this extends to every type of suffering that has afflicted human beings, both present and past.

In chapter 8, I suggested that there are possibly hundreds of thousands of shifters walking anonymously among us at the moment — people who don't have a background in spirituality and so perhaps struggle to make sense of their transformation, never telling anyone about it and perhaps suspecting that they've gone mad. And it's highly likely that this has always been the case, in every human society in every part of the world, in every century throughout history. The only historical spiritual awakenings we know about are those of religious mystics — like the Spanish mystics St. John of the Cross and St. Teresa of Ávila or the British poet-mystics Henry Vaughan and Thomas Traherne — but I'm sure that countless unknown awakenings happened to poor, uneducated people who were unable to preserve their experiences in writing. (It is also certain that, even if they didn't undergo full-fledged transformation, a large portion of them underwent some degree of PTG.)

The Future Evolution of the Human Race

In this last section of this book I would like to turn away from the past and toward the human race's future. I would like to end with some speculations about how the shifters' experiences relate to our future as a species. These are conclusions that have emerged from my fifteen years of research on spiritual awakening — in particular, my research on transformation through turmoil.

To me, it's impossible to separate spiritual awakening from the evolution of consciousness. In a sense, spiritual awakening *is* the evolution of human consciousness. Ever since the first single-celled life-forms appeared on the surface of this planet (which most scientists believe was about four billion years ago), there has been a parallel movement toward increasing physical complexity and increasing *consciousness*. Life-forms have become gradually more aware of their surroundings, more intelligent and sentient, with more complex minds and a deeper understanding of the world around them and of their own selves. In these terms, evolution is a process by which life-forms become increasingly conscious and aware, both of the world and of themselves.

Spiritual awakening is a continuation of this process. Spiritual awakening means attaining a more expansive and intense awareness. When people have temporary awakening experiences, they become more intensely aware of the world around them, more intensely aware of their connection to other living beings (including other human beings) and to nature, and more intensely aware of their own inner being. The same holds true when shifters attain a permanent state of wakefulness. They perceive an intensely real world, with an intense empathic connection to other beings and to nature. They become aware of a new energetic richness within their own being and gain a more expansive conceptual awareness (which isn't so evident in awakening experiences, simply because people tend to be more preoccupied with their perceptions and feelings than with conceptual issues). The shifters' expanded conceptual awareness brings a transcendence of group identity and a sense of connection with and unconditional love toward all human beings, despite any superficial differences of ethnicity and nationality.

In other words, when shifters undergo awakening, it represents an evolutionary progression. Ultimately, their shifts are due to the process of evolution, working through them, continuing its process of moving life-forms to more expansive and intense levels of awareness.

It doesn't often occur to us that evolution stretches in front of us as well as behind us. We tend to unconsciously assume that we human beings (in our present state) represent the *end point* of the evolutionary process. But this is completely illogical, of course. The process of the intensification and expansion of awareness began hundreds of millions of years ago, and it will undoubtedly continue into the future. In fact, we know it is continuing because it is happening right now, manifesting in the shifters' transformations.

Signs of Collective Awakening

Throughout my research on TTT, I've always been struck by how easily and naturally the shifters' higher self emerges. It's as if the higher self is already fully formed and integrated, ready to emerge, just as a chick is ready to hatch from an egg. I think this is because, from an evolutionary point of view, this higher self is the natural unfolding of the next stage in the expansion (and intensification) of awareness on this planet.

It's also significant that, as I pointed out in chapter 8, in every single case of TTT, it is the *same* higher self that emerges. This suggests that we are dealing with a stage of development that has already established itself as a structure and that is inevitably unfolding and revealing itself. There is a parallel with our own development as human beings, from birth to adulthood. Physically and mentally, we move through stages of development that are latent inside us and that unfold naturally and inevitably. I believe that, in a similar way, the state of wakefulness is unfolding in the human race collectively.

In other words, the higher-functioning state of the shifters may be lying in wait for *all* human beings. In a sense, the shifters are harbingers of a new phase of human development, the next phase in the process of the evolution of consciousness on this planet. The new self that is born inside them, during moments of intense turmoil, is waiting to be born within the human race collectively.

I believe that this collective shift may be imminent. It is possible that as a species we are, at the present time, heading toward an evolutionary leap. The impetus of the state of wakefulness appears to be building up within our collective consciousness.

Let me point to three different indications of this. First, there is evidence that awakening experiences — in which we temporarily touch into the state of wakefulness — are becoming more common. In a 1962 Gallup poll, 22 percent of Americans reported that they had "a religious or mystical experience." In 1994, 33 percent of people answered yes to the same question, while in 2009 the figure rose to 49 percent. Research by the Pew Research Center has shown a similar trend. In 2007, 52 percent of Americans reported that they regularly felt a "deep sense of spiritual peace and well-being." In 2014, the figure rose to 59 percent. In 2007, 39 percent of Americans said that they regularly felt a "deep sense of wonder about the universe" — a figure that increased to 46 percent in 2014.

In a 1969 UK survey, people were asked the question, "Have you ever experienced a presence or power, whether or not you call it God, that is different from your everyday self?" Only 29 percent of respondents answered affirmatively, but over the next three decades the figure rose sharply, standing at 75 percent in 2000.

Of course, it could simply be that more people are becoming more aware of — and more accepting of — spiritual experiences. In the past, people were perhaps more likely to repress them or to fail to identity them. But it is also possible that the experiences actually *are* becoming more common.

This ties in with another indication of a collective shift — the massive growth of interest in spirituality and self-development. The human potential movement originally emerged in the 1960s, primarily in the United States and Europe. In recent decades, it has grown at an exponential rate. More and more people feel an impulse to investigate spiritual practices, such as mindfulness or traditional meditation. More and more people feel the urge to follow spiritual paths such as Buddhism, Taoism, and the Kabbalah. More and more people feel the impulse to experiment with psychedelic substances as a way of intensifying and expanding their awareness. It's as if, after centuries of focusing on the external world, striving to control nature and to find happiness in material goods and status, we are turning our attention in the opposite direction. We're starting to explore the *inner* world, and to touch into our potential for growth and transformation. Of course, this may be one reason spiritual experiences are becoming more common, since following spiritual practices and paths obviously makes spiritual experiences more likely.

The third indication is more tentative, relating specifically to this book. After nearly fifteen years spent studying TTT, I am constantly amazed at the numbers of shifters I connect with. Contact with one shifter always seems to lead to contact with several others. Almost every week someone writes to me via my website to tell me that they have undergone a sudden spiritual awakening in the midst of psychological turmoil (often saying that they didn't fully understand what had happened to them before reading my books). I don't have any hard evidence that TTT is becoming more common, although I'm sure that it is more prevalent than most people realize. But it wouldn't surprise me if the experience has become more common over the past few decades or so, in parallel with the two other trends I have described.

The above three factors could be signs that the momentum of wakefulness is increasing and beginning to unfold as the next stage in the evolution of consciousness on this planet. As it unfolds, it is manifesting itself more and more prominently in different aspects of human experience, just as a rising water level manifests itself in different forms, such as overflowing rivers and lakes and new streams and tributaries. Wakefulness is rising and showing signs of its emergence everywhere.

The Necessity of Collective Awakening

It's probably no coincidence that this evolutionary shift is occurring at a time when we urgently need to awaken. Without a collective awakening, our present civilization may not survive. It is even possible that our species may not survive.

We are living through a time of unprecedented crisis. We are suffering from a host of environmental problems, many of which have already reached a critical point: global warming, the mass extinction of other species, water shortage and desertification (leading to mass population movements), the depletion of resources, and so on. The coronavirus pandemic has also caused great devastation, and different strains of the virus may continue to affect us for years to come. These issues are exacerbated by the world's ever-increasing population, and by political and economic instability.

It is impossible for us to solve these problems in our normal sleep state. After all, the problems have been *caused* by our sleep state. Our environmental problems ultimately stem from our ego-separateness, which creates a sense of disconnection from the natural world and an inability to empathize — or feel any sense of responsibility toward — natural phenomena, including nonhuman life-forms. Our fragile separate egos create a desire for wealth and power and for group identity, leading to competition and conflict. Our automatic, familiarized perception of the world edits out the beauty and vividness of our surroundings, causing us to retreat into a claustrophobic world of abstraction inside our heads. The narrowness of our conceptual awareness means that we can't grasp the significance of wide-ranging global problems, only local problems that affect us immediately and directly.

To paraphrase Einstein's reputed statement, we can't solve problems in the same state of consciousness that created them. The only way to solve these problems is to collectively develop a different state of consciousness — that is, to undergo a collective awakening.

We need to wake up to develop a new relationship to the natural world, and to our planet as a whole. We need to wake up so that we no longer waste our lives chasing after trivial and unfulfilling goals such as wealth, status, and success. Once we transcend ego-separation we will no longer feel the impulse to accumulate. Instead, our strongest impulse will be to *contribute*. We need to wake up so that we can move beyond group identity and the conflicts it creates. In part, the future existence of our species depends on our transcending distinctions of nationality and religion and sensing the essential oneness and sameness of all human beings.

In other words, we need to wake up to survive. As Sri Aurobindo put it, "If humanity is to survive, a radical transformation of human nature is indispensable."[1]

Perhaps this is partly *why* we are beginning to wake up. To some extent, our collective awakening may be a survival impulse, triggered by the dangers we are facing. At the same time, our crises may themselves be having an awakening effect. Throughout this book we have seen that turmoil and suffering can transform us as individuals. This is no doubt true in a collective sense too. The impetus of wakefulness may be building up in response to the crises we are facing.

More specifically, this may be related to threats to our survival as a species, or at least to the survival of our present civilization. We have seen that encountering death can have a powerful awakening effect on individuals. And this may well be true for us as a species too. As we face up to the very real danger of ecological catastrophe, we may be collectively undergoing the same type of shift that cancer patients undergo when they are told they may only have a few months left to live.

Above all, this is a question of time. Will we undergo a collective awakening before cataclysmic events occur? Can we wake up in time to rectify the damage we have caused and avert major natural disasters? To a large extent, the answer is in our own hands. Even if we don't undergo TTT, we can consciously cultivate spiritual awakening through practices and paths (such as those I outlined in the last chapter). And in doing so, we can contribute to the collective awakening of our species. The more we awaken as individuals, the more the collective momentum of wakefulness will build up, moving our whole species closer to wakefulness.

And that will be the most extraordinary awakening of all.

APPENDIX

The Characteristics of Wakefulness

ASPECT OF WAKEFULNESS	CHARACTERISTICS
Perceptual	Intensified perception / increased ability to be present Awareness of "Presence" or spiritual energy Aliveness, harmony, and connectedness
Affective	Inner quietness / less identification with thoughts Transcendence of separation / sense of connection Empathy and compassion Well-being Absence of (or decreased) fear of death
Conceptual/ Cognitive	Lack of group identity Wide perspective — universal outlook Heightened sense of morality Appreciation and curiosity
Behavioral	Altruism Enjoyment of inactivity / ability to "be" Nonmaterialism Autonomy / living more authentically Enhanced relationships

ACKNOWLEDGMENTS

Extraordinary Awakenings has been a collaboration with many inspiring and generous people who have allowed me to tell their stories. I would like to send my heartfelt thanks to Gus Hales, Gary, David Wright, Ted, Phyllis, Christopher Wilkinson, Adrian Troy, Ananta Kranti, Edward Little, Suzy, Renee, Mirtha, Graham Stew, LeeAnn Jones, Mark Nepo, Emma Cowing, Jane Metcalfe, David Ditchfield, Zak Khan, Donna Thomas, Parker, Simon, Greg, Eve, Amber, and Nikki Phelan. My thanks also to Sam Sutton of the Prison Phoenix Trust, Marianne Rankin of the Alister Hardy Trust, Lionel Pires, Michael Kaiser (Edward Little's lawyer), and Matthew Green (who put me in touch with Gus). Thanks to Jules Evans for the information from surveys of spiritual experiences. Finally, thanks to Krisztina Egato-Szabo, who helped me as a research assistant in 2017–2018 and provided invaluable support with my study of the transformational effects of bereavement.

NOTES

Introduction

1. See Taylor, "Transformation through Loss and Grief."
2. The Polish psychologist Kazimierz Dąbrowski developed a similar theory in the 1960s. In his studies of "positive disintegration," Dąbrowski discussed how turmoil and suffering often lead to psychological growth. Psychological tension, self-doubt, anxiety, and depression can lead to the breakdown of old personality structure, allowing a new, more integrated personality to develop. Dąbrowski, *Positive Disintegration*.
3. Occasionally, I have also used the term *post-traumatic transformation*. This makes it clear that TTT is associated with — and could be seen as a variant of — post-traumatic growth. However, the term is perhaps a little misleading. *Post* means "after," but many people experience transformation while they are *in the midst of* psychological turmoil rather than afterward. Post-traumatic growth does occur gradually in the aftermath of trauma. While this is sometimes also true of TTT, it is more likely to occur dramatically and suddenly, during a period of intense turmoil.

1. Peace in the Midst of War

1. James, "Moral Equivalent of War," 4.
2. Prabhupada, "Room Conversation."

3. Unfortunately, Karlfried Graf Dürckheim is a good example of the difference between having an awakening experience and being awakened (on an ongoing basis). In the 1930s Dürckheim was affiliated with the Nazis, serving as the Nazi ambassador to Japan. He made a bizarre attempt to reconcile Zen with Nazi ideology. This would have been impossible if he had been genuinely awakened, since wakefulness means transcending group identity and feeling a sense of connection and compassion toward all human beings indiscriminately.

4. In *The Leap*, I used the concepts of the "secondary shift" and the "primary shift" to describe the difference between the transformative effects of awakening experiences and the full-fledged transformation of spiritual awakening.

5. Maguen et al., "Posttraumatic Growth among Gulf War I Veterans."

6. Pietrzak et al., "Posttraumatic Growth in Veterans."

2. Freedom in Prison, Part One

1. Sledge, Boydstun, and Rabe, "Self-Concept Changes."

2. Solomon and Dekel, "Posttraumatic Stress Disorder."

3. Murray, *Evidence of Things Not Seen*, 88.

4. Murray, *Evidence of Things Not Seen*, 97.

5. Murray, *Evidence of Things Not Seen*, 97.

6. Murray, *Evidence of Things Not Seen*, 97.

7. Murray, *Evidence of Things Not Seen*, 96.

8. Murray, *Evidence of Things Not Seen*, 101.

9. Koestler, *Invisible Writing*, 353.

10. Koestler, *Invisible Writing*, 353.

11. Mihajlov, "Freedom in the Gulag."

12. Mihajlov, "Freedom in the Gulag."

13. Mihajlov, "Freedom in the Gulag."

14. Frankl, "Man's Search," 85.

15. Panin, *Notebooks of Sologdin*, 240.

16. Read the full text of this poem here: https://juicyecumenism.com/2017/07/11/irina-ratushinskaya-poet-of-the-valiant-heart.

17. Keay, "Unquenchable Spirit."

18. Read the full text of this poem here: https://dissidentpoetry.wordpress.com/2017/04/05/i-will-live-and-survive.

19. Keay, "Unquenchable Spirit."

20. Aurobindo, *Future Evolution of Man*, 11.

21. Aurobindo, *Letters on Yoga*.
22. Aurobindo, *Tales of Prison Life*, 1.
23. Aurobindo, *Tales of Prison Life*, 49.
24. Aurobindo, *Tales of Prison Life*, 49.
25. Aurobindo, *Tales of Prison Life*, 51.
26. I went through an ascetic period in my own life, when I was about twenty. Impulsively — without any conscious intent or understanding of what I was trying to do — I withdrew from the world, spending almost all my time indoors, rarely meeting anyone. I usually stayed up until four or five o'clock in the morning and got up in the early afternoon. I lived with the bare minimum of possessions, just some clothes, a few books, and some notebooks to write in. I made myself as uncomfortable as possible, sleeping in a sleeping bag on the floor and leaving the windows wide open in the winter. Sometimes I took cold baths and fasted. I also went through a period of self-harming, when I would burn my wrists and arms with a cigarette, hold my fingers in candle flames, and occasionally cut myself. I had a very strong impulse to make life difficult for myself. Certainly, this behavior — particularly my self-harming — was partly caused by frustration, depression, and self-hatred. But overall I believe that my ascetic way of life had a spiritual impulse. I was trying to pare myself down to my essence. I was trying to put myself through the same process of purgation or purification that many mystics and yogis go through consciously, and which some prisoners undergo involuntarily.

3. Freedom in Prison, Part Two

1. In Rankin, *An Introduction*, 224–25.
2. All these quotes come from newsletters of the Prison Phoenix Trust, available at https://www.theppt.org.uk/about-us/newsletters.
3. Alister, *Bombs, Bliss*, 171.
4. "'Hope Is a Powerful Weapon.'"

4. The Greatest Loss

1. From https://www.sacred-texts.com/bud/btg/btg85.htm.
2. Shuchter, *Dimensions of Grief*.
3. Frantz, Trolley, and Farrell, "Positive Aspects."
4. Klass, "Spiritual Aspects," 264.
5. Parappully et al., "Thriving after Trauma."

6. Taylor, *Out of the Darkness*, 55.

7. Taylor, *The Leap*, 117.

8. Taylor, *The Leap*, 117.

9. Taylor, "Transformation through Loss," 6.

10. Tolle, *Power of Now*, 2.

11. Keen, Murray, and Payne, "Sensing the Presence."

12. Roser, "Mortality in the Past."

13. In Barker, *Wordsworth*, 111.

14. In fact, they seem to have had the opposite effect and to have brought about a "spiritual closure" in Wordsworth. One of the puzzling things about Wordsworth is that, although he lived until the age of eighty and wrote hundreds of poems, all his best poetry was written before the age of forty. Critics generally agree that he wrote little of any real merit after this and have often puzzled over the decline in the quality of his work. His later poems lack so much of the freshness and insight of his earlier work that they seem to come from a different author. My view is that this was the result of his grief, beginning with the loss of his brother and later with the loss of his children. One critic wrote that it was as if Wordsworth "iced over," and this was probably due to the trauma of his bereavements.

5. Waking Up to Life through Death

1. Joseph, *What Doesn't Kill Us*.

2. Cowing, "Five Years Ago."

3. Cowing, "Five Years Ago."

4. Kastner, "Beyond Breast Cancer."

5. Stanton, Bower, and Low, "Posttraumatic Growth after Cancer"; Tomich and Helgeson, "Is Finding Something."

6. Taylor, *Out of the Darkness*, 145.

7. Another example is the rock musician Wilko Johnson, whose story I told in *The Leap*.

8. "After Cancer Jolt."

9. E. Kelly and E. Kelly, *Irreducible Mind*.

10. Van Lommel, *Consciousness beyond Life*.

11. Bhagavad-Gita, 53.

12. "A Bright Yellow Light."

13. Renz, *Dying*, 40.

14. Renz, *Dying*, 15.

7. Release from Craving

1. *Alcoholics Anonymous*, 6–7.
2. There is no doubt that many recovering alcoholics do undergo awakenings through following the 12 steps. A 2014 study by researchers at the New York University school of medicine examined the experiences of 161 long-term AA members who reported spiritual awakenings. The majority of awakenings were gradual rather than sudden, and most occurred after "bottoming out." Significantly, two-thirds of the study participants reported that at the present time they had no craving for alcohol or drugs. This suggests that the phenomenon of addiction release is common (Galanter, Dermatis, and Sampson, "Spiritual Awakening").
3. Liebschutz et al., "Relationship between Sexual and Physical Abuse."
4. For two other stories of sudden addiction release, see my book *Out of the Darkness*, chapter 5.

8. Explaining Transformation through Turmoil

1. Many authorities believe that spiritual experiences cannot be described either. This viewpoint probably originated with William James, who stated that one of the characteristics of mystical experiences is that they are "ineffable." However, I think this is an error. Of course mystical experiences can be described! After all, we have read descriptions of them throughout this book. In some cases, they might not be *easy* to describe, but our language is flexible and expansive enough for us to depict them, at least to an extent. And if the experiences prove difficult to convey in ordinary language, we can always use poetry, art, and music to convey them. To some extent, admittedly, it depends on the intensity of the experience. Very intense mystical experiences do go beyond the structures of language. After all, language depends on a duality of subject and object, and on different tenses of time, which are transcended in mystical experiences. But even then, I think the essence of mystical experiences can be conveyed.
2. Another area I would like to investigate is the effect of TTT on dreams. Both David the soldier (in chapter 1) and Parker (in chapter 6) mentioned that they now had regular lucid dreams. It would be interesting to discover how common this is.
3. The transpersonal psychologist Stan Grof has also identified a connection between suicide and spiritual awakening. Based on his psychotherapeutic

work with suicidal patients, Grof has concluded that suicide is the result of a distorted craving for transcendence, a kind of confusion between killing the ego and transcending it. As he puts it, suicide is essentially *egocide* — a term that also applies to spiritual awakening (Grof, *Way of the Psychonaut*).

4. The concept of transliminality was suggested by the psychologist Michael Thalbourne, who suggested that it could explain why some people were more likely to have mystical or psychic experiences than others (Thalbourne and Delin, *Transliminality*). A similar concept of "thin" and "thick" psychological boundaries was developed by Ernest Hartmann in *Boundaries in the Mind*.

5. Taylor, *Out of the Darkness*, 73.

9. Learning from Transformation through Turmoil

1. Frankl, *Man's Search*, 86.
2. Taylor, *The Leap*, 118.

Conclusion

1. Aurobindo, *Future Evolution of Man*, 14.

BIBLIOGRAPHY

"A Bright Yellow Light." BBC Radio, 2019. https://www.bbc.co.uk/programmes
/articles/1c575Zkjg7RDmy3HgdolKrP/a-bright-yellow-light.

"After Cancer Jolt and Four Rounds of Chemo, Clarity Has Come as a
Lightning, Says Irrfan Khan." *Hindustani Times*, August 2, 2018.
https://www.hindustantimes.com/bollywood/after-cancer-jolt-and-four
-rounds-of-chemo-clarity-has-come-as-a-lightning-says-irrfan-khan
/story-yPJsFvbCeBCJjrGoSnPBNN.html.

Alcoholics Anonymous: The Big Book. 1939. Reprint, New York: Alcoholics Anonymous World Services, 2001.

Alister, Paul Narada. *Bombs, Bliss and Baba: The Spiritual Autobiography behind
the Hilton Bombing Frame Up.* Maleny, Australia: Better World Books, 1997.

Aurobindo, Sri. *Tales of Prison Life.* Calcutta: Sri Aurobindo Institute, 1920,
pdf. https://www.auro-ebooks.com/tales-of-prison-life/#:~:text=%20
Tales%20of%20Prison%20Life%20%201%20Tales,the%20%E2%80%9C.

———. *The Future Evolution of Man: The Divine Life upon Earth.* London: Allen
& Unwin, 1963.

———. *Letters on Yoga.* Vol. 1, 1971. https://www.aurobindo.ru/workings/sa
/22/0002_e.htm#ii.

Barker, Juliet. *Wordsworth: A Life in Letters.* London: Penguin, 2003.

Bhagavad-Gita. Edited and translated by Juan Mascaro. London: Penguin, 1988.

Cowing, Emma. "Five Years Ago, I Was Pronounced Dead in Afghanistan. This

Is What I've Learned Since." *The Spectator* (December 2013). https://www
.spectator.co.uk/article/five-years-ago-i-was-pronounced-dead-in
-afghanistan-this-is-what-i-ve-learned-since.

Dąbrowski, Kazimierz. *Positive Disintegration.* Anna Maria, FL: Maurice Bassett,
2016.

Frankl, Viktor E. *Man's Search for Meaning: An Introduction to Logotherapy.*
1946. Reprint, New York: Simon & Schuster, 1984.

Frantz, Thomas, Barbara Trolley, and Megan Farrell. "Positive Aspects of Grief."
Pastoral Psychology 47, no. 1 (October 2014): 3–17. http://dx.doi.org/10.1023
/A:1022988612298.

Galanter, Marc, Helen Dermatis, and Cristal Sampson. "Spiritual Awakening in
Alcoholics Anonymous: Empirical Findings." *Alcoholism Treatment Quarterly* 32, nos. 2–3 (June 2014): 319–34. doi: 10.1080/07347324.2014.907058.

Grof, Stanislav. *The Way of the Psychonaut.* Vol. 1. Santa Cruz, CA: Multidisci-
plinary Association for Psychedelic Studies, 2019.

Hartmann, Ernest. *Boundaries in the Mind: A New Psychology of Personality.*
New York: Basic Books, 1991.

"'Hope Is a Powerful Weapon': Unpublished Mandela Prison Letters." *New York
Times* Sunday Review, July 6, 2018. https://www.nytimes.com/2018/07/06
/opinion/sunday/nelson-mandela-unpublished-prison-letters-excerpts.html.

James, William. "The Moral Equivalent of War." In *The Moral Equivalent of War,
and Other Essays.* Edited by John K. Roth. New York: Harper & Row, 1971.

Joseph, Stephen. *What Doesn't Kill Us: A Guide to Overcoming Adversity and
Moving Forward.* London: Piatkus, 2013.

Kastner, R. S. "Beyond Breast Cancer Survival: The Meaning of Thriving." *Dis-
sertation Abstracts International: Section B: The Sciences and Engineering* 59,
no. 5–B (November 1998): 2421.

Keay, Kathy. "Unquenchable Spirit: Irina Ratushinskaya RIP." *Thunderstruck*
(July 21, 2017). http://thunderstruck.org/unquenchable-spirit-irina
-ratushinskaya-rip.

Keen, Catherine, Craig D. Murray, and Sheila A. Payne. "Sensing the Presence
of the Deceased: A Narrative Review." *Mental Health, Religion & Culture* 16,
no. 4 (January 2012): 384–402. https://doi.org/10.1080/13674676.2012.678987.

Kelly, Edward, and Emily W. Kelly. *Irreducible Mind: Toward a Psychology for the
21st Century.* Lanham, MD: Rowman & Littlefield, 2007.

Klass, Dennis. "Spiritual Aspects of the Resolution of Grief." In *Dying: Facing the
Facts*, edited by Hannelore Wass and Robert A. Niemeyer, 243–68. Wash-
ington, DC: Taylor & Francis, 1995.

Koestler, Arthur. *The Invisible Writing.* New York: Macmillan, 1954.

Liebschutz, Jane, Jacqueline B. Savetsky, Richard Saitz, Nicholas J. Horton, Christine Lloyd-Travaglini, and Jeffrey H. Samet. "The Relationship between Sexual and Physical Abuse and Substance Abuse Consequences." *Journal of Substance Abuse Treatment* 22, no. 3 (April 2002): 121–28. doi: 10.1016/s0740-5472(02)00220-9.

Maguen, Shira, Dawne Vogt, Daniel W. King, Lynda A. King, and Brett Litz. "Posttraumatic Growth among Gulf War I Veterans: The Predictive Role of Deployment-Related Experiences and Background Characteristics." *Journal of Loss and Trauma* 11, no. 5 (December 2006): 378–88. doi: 10.1080/15325020600672004.

Mandela, Nelson. *Long Walk to Freedom: The Autobiography of Nelson Mandela.* London: Abacus, 1995.

Mihajlov, Mihajlo. "Freedom in the Gulag: Spiritual Lessons of the Concentration Camp." *Crisis Magazine* (November 1, 1988). https://www.crisismagazine.com /1988/freedom-in-the-gulag-spiritual-lessons-of-the-concentration-camp.

Murray, W. H. *The Evidence of Things Not Seen: A Mountaineer's Tale.* London: Baton Wicks, 2002.

Panin, Dimitrii Mikhailovich. *The Notebooks of Sologdin.* New York: Harcourt Brace Jovanovich, 1976.

Parappully, Jose, Robert Rosenbaum, Leland van den Deale, and Esther Nzewi. "Thriving after Trauma: The Experience of Parents of Murdered Children. *Journal of Humanistic Psychology* 42, no. 1 (January 2002): 33–70. https://doi .org/10.1177/0022167802421003.

Pietrzak, Robert H., Marc B. Goldstein, James C. Malley, Alison J. Rivers, Douglas C. Johnson, Charles A. Morgan, and Stephen M. Southwick. "Posttraumatic Growth in Veterans of Operations Enduring Freedom and Iraqi Freedom. *Journal of Affective Disorders* 126, nos. 1–2 (October 2010): 230–35. https://doi.org/10.1016/j.jad.2010.03.021.

Prabhupada, Swami. "Room Conversation with Professor Dürckheim, Dr. P. J. Saher, and Professor Porsch." Interview, June 19, 1974. https://prabhupada .io/spoken/740619r1.ger#id20.

Rankin, Marianne. *An Introduction to Religious and Spiritual Experience.* London: Continuum, 2009.

Renz, Monika. *Dying: A Transition.* New York: Columbia University Press, 2015.

Roser, Max. "Mortality in the Past — Around Half Died as Children." *Our World in Data,* July 11, 2019. https://ourworldindata.org/child-mortality-in-the-past.

Shuchter, Stephen R. *Dimensions of Grief: Adjusting to the Death of a Spouse.* San Francisco: Jossey-Bass, 1986.

Sledge, William H., J. A. Boydstun, and A. J. Rabe. "Self-Concept Changes

Related to War Captivity." *Archives of General Psychiatry* 37, no. 4 (May 1980): 430–43.

Solomon, Zahava, and Rachel Dekel. "Posttraumatic Stress Disorder and Post-traumatic Growth Among Israeli Ex-POWs." *Journal of Traumatic Stress* 20, no. 3 (June 2007): 303–12.

Stanton, Annette L., Julienne E. Bower, and Carissa A. Low. "Posttraumatic Growth after Cancer." In *Handbook of Posttraumatic Growth: Research and Practice*, edited by Lawrence G. Calhoun and Richard G. Tedeschi, 138–75. Mahwah, NJ: Erlbaum, 2006.

Taylor, Steve. *Waking from Sleep: Why Awakening Experiences Occur and How to Make Them Permanent*. London: Hay House, 2010.

———. *Out of the Darkness: From Turmoil to Transformation*. London: Hay House, 2011.

———. *The Leap: The Psychology of Spiritual Awakening*. Novato, CA: New World Library, 2017.

———. "Transformation through Loss and Grief: A Study of Personal Transformation Following Bereavement." *The Humanistic Psychologist* (March 2020). doi: https://doi.org/10.1037/hum0000172.

Taylor, Steve, Divine Charura, Elliot Cohen, Fiona Meth, John Allan, Glenn Williams, Mandy Shaw, and Leonie O'Dwyer. "Loss, Grief, and Growth: An Interpretative Phenomenological Analysis of Experiences of Trauma in Asylum Seekers and Refugees. *Traumatology* (March 2020). https://doi.apa.org/doiLanding?doi=10.1037/trm0000250.

Thalbourne, Michael A., and Peter S. Delin. "Transliminality: Its Relation to Dream Life, Religiosity, and Mystical Experience." *International Journal for the Psychology of Religion* 9, no. 1 (1999): 45–61. doi: 10.1207/s15327582ijpr0901_6.

Tolle, Eckhart. *The Power of Now*. 1997. Reprint, Novato, CA: New World Library, 2004.

Tomich, Patricia L., and Vicki S. Helgeson. "Is Finding Something Good in the Bad Always Good? Benefit Finding among Women with Breast Cancer." *Health Psychology* 23, no. 1 (January 2004): 16–23.

Van Lommel, Pim. *Consciousness beyond Life: The Science of Near-Death Experience*. San Francisco: HarperOne, 2011.

FURTHER SOURCES

David Ditchfield writes extensively about his near-death experience and its effect on his life in his book *Shine On: The Remarkable Story of How I Fell under a Speeding Train, Journeyed to the Afterlife, and the Astonishing Proof I Brought Back with Me* (UK: O-Books, 2020).

Ananta Kranti's website is https://www.ananta-kranti.com. Her latest book is *What Looks through Your Eyes?* (Surrey, UK: Yogaland, 2021).

The website of the Prison Phoenix Trust is https://www.theppt.org.uk.

Donna Thomas's research website is https://childrenselfand anomalousexperiences.co.uk.

If you are undergoing a difficult spiritual awakening, you can contact the Spiritual Crisis Network at https://spiritualcrisis network.uk or the American Center for the Integration of Spiritually Transformative Experiences at https://aciste.org.

If you have undergone transformation through turmoil, you can describe your experience on the "Have you ever had an awakening experience?" forum on my website, https://www.stevenmtaylor.com.

INDEX

ABOUT THE AUTHOR

Steve Taylor, PhD, is the author of several books on psychology and spirituality, including *The Leap* and *Waking from Sleep*. He is also the author of three books of spiritual poetry, including *The Clear Light* and *The Calm Center*, and the audio course *Return to Harmony*. Taylor is a senior lecturer in psychology at Leeds Beckett University in the United Kingdom and writes the popular blog *Out of the Darkness* for *Psychology Today*. He lives in Manchester, England.

A portion of the royalties of this book will be given to organizations that support spiritual awakening in the midst of turmoil, including the Prison Phoenix Trust, which supports the spiritual development of prisoners in the UK and runs meditation and yoga classes.